CONTROLLED SUBSTANCE
OFFENCES

AUSTRALIA
Law Book Co.
Sydney

CANADA and USA
Carswell
Toronto

HONG KONG
Sweet & Maxwell Asia

NEW ZEALAND
Brookers
Wellington

SINGAPORE and MALAYSIA
Sweet & Maxwell Asia
Singapore and Kuala Lumpur

CONTROLLED SUBSTANCE OFFENCES

GENERAL EDITOR

P.W. Ferguson
Advocate

CONTRIBUTORS

Iain Bradley
Solicitor and member of the Procurator Fiscal Service

Robert S. Shiels
Solicitor and member of the Procurator Fiscal Service

THOMSON

W. GREEN

Published in 2003 by

W. Green & Son Ltd
21 Alva Street
Edinburgh EH2 4PS

www.wgreen.co.uk

Printed in Great Britain by Creative Print and Design Group,
Harmondsworth, Middlesex

No natural forests were destroyed to make this product;
Only farmed timber was used and replanted

A CIP catalogue record for this book is available from the British Library

ISBN 0 414 01491 X

Annotations © W. Green & Son Ltd 2003

PREFACE

When Renton and Brown's *Statutory Offences* was first published the aim was to provide, as a complementary work to Sir Gerald Gordon, QC's classic sixth edition on *Criminal Procedure* (which was published in 1996), a thorough and readily available collection of the principal statutory offences grouped, for convenience, according to general subject matter. One such group was Division A which is the subject of this off-print. It has subsequently appeared sensible to produce a separate edition of *Controlled Substance Offences* because, while other divisions such as sexual offences and firearms are equally important, the offences under the relevant statutes are less frequently encountered than those under the Misuse of Drugs Act 1971 which is the main statute treated in Division A.

Prosecutions for offences under the Misuse of Drugs Act 1971 are most often conducted in the sheriff court, usually under summary procedure, but the real and worrying extent of the controlled drugs problem which still besets the Scottish criminal justice system at present can be seen in the number of indictments which are regularly prosecuted in the High Court. The steep rise in such prosecutions was first noted by Lord Maxwell as having occurred in the mid-1980s when the number of drugs offences indictments disposed of in the High Court (as a percentage of the total number of indictments) increased from 6.1 per cent in 1983 to 29.9 per cent in 1985 (see *Report of the Review Body on Use of Judicial Time in the Superior Courts in Scotland* (April 1986, S.C.A.), para.8.17 and Table 16).

The Misuse of Drugs Act 1971 is a United Kingdom statute and is indeed a reserved matter under the Scotland Act 1998 so that alteration of the substance of the law relating to controlled drugs can only be effected by the Westminster Parliament. Thus, this month (though too late for inclusion in this edition) the Westminster Parliament reclassified cannabis and cannabis resin: these now are Class C substances in Schedule 2 of the 1971 Act with a correspondingly lower range of penalties than previously were applicable. Thus also the annotations draw freely from the larger case law of the English superior courts in order to state what the statutory provisions mean. No apology is given or needed for this approach since it is well established that the courts of both jurisdictions should strive to ensure that they give the same interpretation to the same provisions, especially where the liberty of the subject is imperilled, although this is not always inevitable (see *McIntosh v H.M. Advocate*, 1994 S.L.T. 59 at 62; *cf. Cording v Halse* [1955] 1 Q.B. 63 at 70). One explanation for divergence can, however, be pleaded in the Scottish courts' favour: there is a marked tendency for inconsistent decisions to accumulate in England because of the large number of differently constituted courts in the Criminal Division of the Court of Appeal and it is no function of the Scottish courts to rationalise what is ultimately foreign law.

The law is stated as at October 2003.

P.W. Ferguson
Parliament House
Edinburgh

v

CONTENTS

TABLE OF CASES

Table of Cases

TABLE OF STATUTES

TABLE OF STATUTORY INSTRUMENTS

EXPLOSIVE SUBSTANCES ACT 1883

(46 & 47 Vict., C.3)

An Act to amend the law relating to Explosive Substances

[10th April 1883]

GENERAL NOTE

The criminal use of explosives (as distinct from the manufacture and storage of explosives) is governed principally by the Explosive Substances Act 1883 (46 & 47 Vict.), ss.2, 3 and 4. Sections 2 and 3 were amended by s.7 of the Criminal Jurisdiction Act 1975 (c.59) which conferred on the Scottish courts the jurisdiction to try offences committed abroad.

The 1883 Act does not define the expression "explosive substance". The only guidance provided by the Act is s.9(1) which deems the phrase "explosive substance" to include any materials for making any explosive substance, any apparatus, machine or implement or materials used, or intended to be used, or adapted for causing, or aiding in causing, any explosion in or with any explosive substance, and any part of any such apparatus, machine or implement. However, in England, the Court of Appeal has held that the 1883 Act should be construed in the light of the definition of the term "explosive" as it is used in the Explosives Act 1875 (38 & 39 Vict., c.17), s.3 of which provides that "explosive" means gunpowder, nitoglycerine, dynamite, gun-cotton, blasting powders, fulminate of mercury or of other metals, coloured fibres and "every other substance, whether similar to those above mentioned or not, used or manufactured with a view to producing a practical effect by explosion or pyrotechnic effect" (see *R. v Wheatley* (1979) 68 Cr.App.R. 287).

In *McIntosh v H.M. Advocate*, 1994 S.L.T. 59 the High Court did not question the relevancy of a libel which alleged the contravention of s.2 of the 1883 Act by use of petrol bombs made from bottles. In England, such items have been held to be "explosive substances" (*R. v Bouch* (1983) 76 Cr.App.R. 11). In Northern Ireland the phrase has been held to encompass a shotgun (*R. v Downey* [1971] N.I. 224).

Causing explosion likely to endanger life or property

2. A person who in the United Kingdom or (being a citizen of the United Kingdom and Colonies) in the Republic of Ireland unlawfully and maliciously causes by any explosive substance an explosion of a nature likely to endanger life or to cause serious injury to property shall, whether any injury to person or property has been actually caused or not, be guilty of an offence and on conviction on indictment shall be liable to imprisonment for life.

AMENDMENT

Section 2 as amended by the Criminal Jurisdiction Act 1975 (c.59) s7(1).

GENERAL NOTE

There are three requisites for conviction under s.2: (1) that the accused caused an explosion (whether directly or by acting in concert with another); (2) that the explosion was unlawful and malicious; and (3) that the explosion was likely to endanger life or cause serious damage to property. The High Court has held that it is sufficient to satisfy the malicious element of the offence that the accused was reckless and indicated (though the court reserved its opinion on this aspect) that the test of recklessness is, unlike English law, objectively assessed (*McIntosh v H.M. Advocate*, 1994 S.L.T. 59).

1

Attempt to cause explosion, or making or keeping explosive with intent to endanger life or property

3. — (1) A person who in the United Kingdom or a dependency or (being a citizen of the United Kingdom and Colonies) elsewhere unlawfully and maliciously—

(a) does any act with intent to cause, or conspires to cause, by an explosive substance an explosion of a nature likely to endanger life, or cause serious injury to property, whether in the United Kingdom or the Republic of Ireland, or

(b) makes or has in his possession or under his control an explosive substance with intent by means thereof to endanger life, or cause serious injury to property, whether in the United Kingdom or the Republic of Ireland, or to enable any other person so to do,

shall, whether any explosion does or does not take place, and whether any injury to person or property is actually caused or not, be guilty of an offence and on conviction on indictment shall be liable to imprisonment for life, and the explosive substance shall be forfeited.

(2) ...

AMENDMENTS

Section 3 substituted by the Criminal Jurisdiction Act 1975 (c.59), s.7(1).
Subs.(1) as amended by the Criminal Law Act 1977 (c.45) s.33 and Sch.12 and SI 1977/1249, art.5(2).

GENERAL NOTE

Maliciously. Although in *McIntosh v H.M. Advocate*, 1994 S.L.T. 59, the High Court held that "maliciously" in s.2 was in law to be taken to include recklessness as a sufficient *mens rea* as well as meaning intentionally, the use of the word in s.3 does not appear to be capable of such breadth and might in fact be meaningless given the references in paras (a) and (b) to the doing of acts with intent. Moreover, the reference in para.(a) to conspiracy must exclude mere recklessness since conspiracy requires agreement (*Maxwell v H.M. Advocate*, 1980 J.C. 40) and must accordingly be a crime of intent shared by two or more persons.

A person who. It is unnecessary that the accused be present within the United Kingdom when the acts were done in breach of the section (see *R. v Ellis* (1992) 95 Cr.App.R. 52).

Dependency. Subsection (2) defined dependency as the Channel Islands, the Isle of Man and any colony other than a colony for whose external relations a country other than the United Kingdom is responsible.

Punishment for making or possession of explosive under suspicious circumstances.

4. — (1) Any person who makes or knowingly has in his possession or under his control any explosive substance, under such circumstances as to give rise to a reasonable suspicion that he is not making it or does not have it in his possession or under his control for a lawful object, shall, unless he can show that he made it or had it in his possession or under his control for a lawful object, be guilty of [an offence], and, liable to imprisonment for a term not exceeding 14 years and the explosive substance shall be forfeited.

(2) ...

AMENDMENT

Subs.(1) as amended by the Criminal Procedure (Scotland) Act 1975 (c.21), s.221(1).

GENERAL NOTE

Knowingly has in his possession or under his control. In *Black v H.M. Advocate*, 1974 J.C. 43;

1974 S.L.T. 247 the High Court held that the Crown required to prove that the accused either possessed the explosives or that he knew of their presence in premises which he controlled, or at least that the accused had permitted the introduction of the explosive to his premises or connived at the explosives remaining there.

Reasonable suspicion. The suspicion which the possession of the explosive (or the having of the explosive under one's control) must give rise to is to be assessed objectively by the jury in the light of the proved circumstances of the accused's possession or exercising of control.

Lawful object In England it has been held that the possession of explosives for the purposes of self defence is a lawful object, but it is open to doubt whether such a view (which ultimately depends on public poicy grounds) would be followed in Scots law. While the 1883 Act is a United Kingdom statute (see Criminal Jurisdiction Act 1975, s.7(3)) the High Court in *McIntosh v H.M. Advocate*, 1994 S.L.T. 59, observed that s.2 had to be construed in terms of Scots law. Presumably the same approach would be adopted to s.4 and that being so, it is likely that on public policy grounds the High Court would regard the possession of explosives (at least in the general sense of that expression though perhaps not in the extended meaning of the word) as an excessive form of self defence. In any event, the decision in *Attorney-General's Reference (No. 2 of 1983)* [1984]. Q.B. 456 which holds that self defence can be a lawful object, appears to run into the difficulty in Scots law that self defence is only available to an accused who has no other reasonable means of avoiding the threatened harm.

The lawful object need not be an object which is intended to be met in Scotland (or the United Kingdom) but can be one which is intended to be met in a foreign country. In such a case the lawfulness which the accused must prove on balance of probabilities requires to be proved by reference to the law of the foreign country (see *R. v Berry* [1985] A.C. 246).

Unless he can show The accused bears the burden of proving on a balance of probabilities that the object of his possession or control was lawful (*Attorney-General's Reference (No. 2 of 1983)*). The accused is not required, however, to adduce corroborated evidence (see *King v Lees*, 1993 S.L.T. 1184 at 1187F). Whether this legal burden should be "read down" under s.3 of the Human Rights Act 1998 is a moot point.

MISUSE OF DRUGS ACT 1971

(1971 c.38)

An Act to make new provision with respect to dangerous or other wise harmful drugs and related matters, and for purposes connected therewith.
[27th May 1971]

GENERAL NOTE

Prior to the twentieth century there was no comprehensive legislative regulation of non-medicinal drugs. There were various statutes directed to certain drugs but it was not until the passing of the Drugs (Prevention of Misuse) Act 1964 (c.64) that a thorough attempt at control of non-medicinal use of drugs was commenced. The present law is contained in the 1971 Act which attempts to deal comprehensively with a wide variety of drugs. These drugs are described as "controlled drugs" (s.2) and under the 1971 Act are divided into three classes, namely Classes A, B and C, which are specified in Parts I, II and III respectively of Sch.2 to the 1971 Act. A drug may be added to or removed from the schedule (or moved from one Class to another Class) by Order in Council. The importance of classification of a controlled drug lies in the penalties which the 1971 Act applies to offences in relation to them. There have been several Orders in Council modifying Sch.2 since the passing of the 1971 Act (on May 27, 1971), the most recent of which having come into force on May 1, 1998 adding a further six substances to the schedule (see the Misuse of Drugs Act 1971 (Modification) Order 1998 (SI 1998 No. 750)).

The 1971 Act creates offences which fall into three broad categories. Importation and exportation of controlled drugs is struck at by the statutory declaration in s.3 (although the breach of the prohibition is prosecuted under the Customs and Excise Management Act 1979 (see *infra*). The second range of offences relates to production and supply (including cultivation). The third type of offence is possession (including possession with intent to supply). At this stage it is appropriate to notice that all cases of misuse of controlled drugs are, with one exception, prosecuted under statute. The one exception arises where death results. Where, for example, A supplied B with a controlled drug in an adulterated condition or in an excessive or perhaps even lethal quantity, and B died as a result of ingesting the controlled drug in entirety, a charge of criminal homicide will be relevant. If the Crown can prove that A's intention in making the supply was to bring about death (or that A was wickedly reckless as to whether death would result) then A can be liable for murder. Where, however, A's mental state was not murderously reckless he can be liable for culpable homicide. In either case it is irrelevant that B voluntarily ingested the controlled drug: B's act does not constitute a *novus actus interveniens* (see *Lord Advocate's Reference (No. 1 of 1994)*, 1995 S.L.T. 248; 1995 S.C.C.R. 177).

...

Controlled Drugs and their Classification

Controlled Drugs and their Classification for Purposes of this Act.

2. — (1) In this Act—
(a)   the expression "controlled drug" means any substance or product for the time being specified in Part I, II, or III of Schedule 2 to this Act; and
(b)   the expressions "Class A drug", "Class B drug" and "Class C drug" mean any of the substances and products for the time being specified respectively in Part I, Part II and Part III of that Schedule;
and the provisions of Part IV of that Schedule shall have effect with respect to the meanings of expressions used in that Schedule.

(2)   Her Majesty may by Order in Council make such amendments in Schedule 2 to this Act as may be requisite for the purpose of adding any substance or product to, or removing any substance or product from, any of Parts I to III of that Schedule, including amendments for securing that no substance or product is for the time being specified in a particular one of those Parts or for inserting any substance or product into any of those Parts in which no substance or product is for the time being specified.

(3)   An Order in Council under this section may amend Part IV of Schedule 2 to this Act, and may do so whether or not it amends any other Part of that Schedule.

(4)   An Order in Council under this section may be varied or revoked by a subsequent Order in Council thereunder.

(5)   No recommendation shall be made to Her Majesty in Council to make an Order under this section unless a draft of the Order has been laid before Parliament and approved by a resolution of each House of Parliament; and

the Secretary of State shall not lay a draft of such an Order before Parliament except after consultation with or on the recommendation of the Advisory Council.

GENERAL NOTE

Substance or product. The reference to substance or product in the definition of "controlled drug" is significant when content is sought to be given to the statutory defence set out in s.28(3) (see *Salmon v H.M. Advocate; Moore v H.M. Advocate*, 1999 S.L.T. 169 at 173F; 1998 S.C.C.R. 740 at 748C, *per* Lord Justice-General Rodger).

Consultation with or on the recommendation of the Advisory Council. Section 1 of the 1971 Act creates an Advisory Council on the Misuse of Drugs (the details of its constitution, etc. being set forth in Sch.1 to the Act). Any Order in Council amending the list of controlled drugs requires, as a condition precedent, to have been referred to the Advisory Council before it can be laid before Parliament (s.2(5)).

Restrictions Relating to Controlled Drugs, etc.

Restriction of Importation and Exportation of Controlled Drugs

3. — (1) Subject to subsection (2) below—
(a)   the importation of a controlled drug; and
(b)   the exportation of a controlled drug,
are hereby prohibited.
(2)   Subsection (1) above does not apply—
(a)   to the importation of exportation of a controlled drug which is for the time being excepted from paragraph (a) or, as the case may be, paragraph (b) of subsection (1) above by regulations under Section 7 of this Act; or
(b)   to the importation or exportation of a controlled drug under and in accordance with the terms of a licence issued by the Secretary of State and in compliance with any conditions attached thereto.

GENERAL NOTE

The importation and exportation of controlled drugs as defined in s.2, are prohibited generally but s.7(1)(a) empowers the Secretary of State for the Home Department (and in Northern Ireland, the Minister for Home Affairs) to provide exceptions which exclude specified controlled drugs from the prohibition. This section does not provide for contravention of the prohibition being punishable as a criminal offence. That is achieved by s.170(2)(b) of the Customs and Excise Management Act 1979 (c.2) (see *infra*).

Restriction of Production and Supply of Controlled Drugs

4. — (1) Subject to any regulations under Section 7 of this Act for the time being in force, it shall not be lawful for a person—
(a)   to produce a controlled drug; or
(b)   to supply or offer to supply a controlled drug to another.
(2)   Subject to Section 28 of this Act, it is an offence for a person—
(a)   to produce a controlled drug in contravention of subsection (1) above; or
(b)   to be concerned in the production of such a drug in contravention of that subsection by another.
(3)   Subject to Section 28 of this Act, it is an offence for a person—
(a)   to supply or offer to supply a controlled drug to another in contravention of subsection (1) above; or
(b)   to be concerned in the supplying of such a drug to another in contravention of that subsection; or

(c) to be concerned in the making to another in contravention of that subsection of an offer to supply such a drug.

General Note

Section 4 along with s.5 contains the principal criminal offences in relation to the enforcement of the controlled drugs regime. Subsections (2) and (3) render it criminal to produce or supply or offer to supply a controlled drug as well as to be concerned in the production of a controlled drug or in the making to another of an offer to supply a controlled drug. The most commonly encountered charge is one under subs.(3)(b), being concerned in the supplying of a controlled drug to another, although it is sometimes employed in cases where the appropriate offence should be a contravention of s.5(3) (see dictum of Lord Justice-General Rodger in *Salmon v H.M. Advocate; Moore v H.M. Advocate*, 1999 S.L.T. 169 at 181A–B and 182D).

See the discussion of the suggested misapplication of s.4(3)(b) charges to factual circumstances appropriately charged under s.5(3): K. Bovey, "Section 4(3)(b) of the Misuse of Drugs Act 1971", 2000 Crim.L.B. 45–2.

In *Cochrane v H.M. Advocate*, May 13, 1999 (unreported); 1999 G.W.D. 20–927, the Appeal Court reserved their opinion on the question whether, on a proper construction of their terms, the charges under s.4(3)(b) and s.5(3) were mutually exclusive because there was evidence against the appellant extending beyond possession with intent to supply and the jury were accordingly entitled on any view to convict him of being concerned in supplying. The court, however, described the point as "a matter of some substance". The point arose again in the Appeal Court in *McCutcheon v H. M. Advocate*, May 11, 2001 (unreported) but for the same reason that the evidence did not raise a live issue as to the scope of s.4(3)(b), the court declined to decide the point. However, Temporary Judge Sir G.H. Gordon, QC has held in *H.M Advocate v Kiernan*, 2001 S.C.C.R. 129, in repelling a submission of no case to answer, that the Crown were entitled to charge a person who was in possession of controlled drugs with intent to supply them to another person (even if that other were not himself a consumer) with a contravention of either s.5(3) or s.4(3)(b), at their option (at 132G (para.10)).

Production of or supply (or offer to supply) a controlled drug is declared to be unlawful subject to the Secretary of State's powers under s.7(1) by regulations to except certain specified controlled drugs (subs. (1)(a)) and to render it lawful for persons to do things which would otherwise be unlawful for them to do by virtue of ss.4(1), 5(1) and 6(1) of the 1971 Act (subs. (1)(b)). These regulations may license the doing of such things or permit things to be done subject to conditions (s.7(2)). Section 7(3)(a) empowers the Secretary of State to provide by regulation that it shall not be unlawful for doctors, dentists and veterinary practitioners (and surgeons) to prescribe, administer, manufacture, compound or supply a controlled drug (or for a pharmacist or a person lawfully conducting a retail pharmacy business (see s.37(5)) to manufacture, compound or supply a controlled drug, so long as each such person does so "in his capacity as such" professional person. Section 7(3)(b) allows the Secretary of State to render lawful such persons having in their possession a controlled drug so long as such possession is for the purpose of acting in their capacity as a professional person. The power to make regulations has been exercised: see Misuse of Drugs Regulations 1985 (SI 1985/2066).

An important provision in the 1985 Regulations is reg.10(2) which provides that notwithstanding the prohibition in s.5(1), a person may have in his possession any drug specified in Schedule 2 or 3 "for administration for medical, dental or veterinary purposes in accordance with the directions of a practitioner." (The dispensation does not apply, however, where the patient has not told his doctor that he has already been supplied with any controlled drug by another doctor or where he has made a false declaration or statement for the purpose of obtaining the supply or prescription.) It is for the accused to put in issue his lawful possession under reg.10(2) (*Wood v Allan*, 1988 S.L.T. 341; 1988 S.C.C.R. 115).

Production. Section 37(1) provides that producing a controlled drug means producing it by manufacture, cultivation or any other method. It has been held in England that the phrase "any other method" in s.37(1) is habile to encompass the preparation of cannabis plants by discarding the parts which are not usable and the putting together of those parts which are usable (*R. v Harris* [1996] 1 Cr.App.R. 369). It has also been held to be production for an accused to convert cocaine hydrochloride into "crack" cocaine, which are both Class A drugs but separately identifiable by chemical means (*R. v Russell* (1992) 94 Cr.App.R. 351).

Being concerned in the production. The expression "being concerned" when used in the context of supply of a controlled drug (under s.4(3)(b)) has been given a wide meaning (see *Kerr v H.M. Advocate*, 1986 S.C.C.R. 81; 1986 J.C. 41) such that it has been suggested that there is no room for an accused's being art and part in an offence of being concerned in the supply of a controlled

8

drug (see *Salmon v H.M. Advocate; Moore v H.M. Advocate*, 1999 S.L.T. 169 at 182G–H and 187H). There is no reason in principle for the same view not to be applied in charges under s.4(2)(b). For an unusual case where the Court of Appeal in England quashed a conviction under s.4(2), see *R. v Farr* [1982] Crim. L.R. 745.

Supply. Section 37(1) contains no exhaustive definition of "supplying" but provides that it includes distributing. For the offence of offering to supply a controlled drug to be complete it is unnecessary to prove that the accused intended to fulfil the offer (*R. v Gill* (1992) 97 Cr.App.R. 215; *R. v Goodard* [1992] Crim. L.R. 588; *R. v Showers* [1995] Crim. L.R. 400).

It has been held in the Court of Appeal (Crim Div.) in *R. v Dhillon* [2000] T.L.R. 266 that in a charge of offering to supply a controlled drug, it was wrong to introduce the principles of the law of contract. Thus the court rejected the contention that once an offer to supply had been made to an undercover police officer and had been accepted by him, the offer fell and could not be regarded as a continuing offer.

What is essential is a transfer of physical control of a controlled drug from one person to another (see *Donnelly v H.M. Advocate*, 1985 S.L.T. 243 approving *R. v Delgado* [1984] 1 W.L.R. 89 at 92) when supply is in issue although it it is not essential that the supply be made out of the accused's own resources (see *R. v Maginnis* [1987] 2 W.L.R. 765). In *Maginnis, supra,* the House of Lords held that more than mere transfer of physical possession was needed: supply requires the additional concept of enabling the recipient to apply the drug handed over to purposes for which the recipient desires or has a duty to apply it but it is undecided in Scots law whether such an additional concept is necessary.

It has been held in the Court of Appeal (Crim. Div.) in *R v Panton* [2001] T.L.R. 240 that the meaning of "supply" applied notwithstanding lack of consent on the part of the keeper with whom the drugs were deposited and that, accordingly, where the accused had acted as involuntary keeper of the drugs, so long as the jury rejected the defence of duress (if it was raised), the fact that the accused (who alleged that he had received the drugs after being subjected to threats) had intended to return the drugs to their depositors was irrelevant on a charge under s.5(3). This is almost certainly the position under Scots law—see below.

Defence of coercion. The defence is a general one and available in all charges (with one possible exception: see Gordon, *Criminal Law* (3rd ed. by M.G.A. Christie), Vol. I, para.13.29; Ferguson, *Crimes Against The Person* (2nd ed.), para.13.18). However, there are two important limitations on the availability of the defence. First, the accused must not fail to take any reasonable step to nullify the threat to himself or a third party if he is to be able to found on coercion. Thus, in *Trotter v H.M. Advocate*, 2000 S.C.C.R. 968, where the accused gave evidence that he had heroin in his possession when visiting his father in prison because he had been threatened that if he did not deliver it to his father, his father would be stabbed and that if he told anyone, he would be stabbed, the Appeal Court held that the defence was incapable of being maintained on a charge under s.5(3) because the accused had chosen not to inform the authorities. Lord Reed said: "Such circumstances cannot amount to a complete defence to a criminal charge, although they may, if accepted, be taken into account in mitigation of sentence." (at 972B–C (para.4)). The same view has been taken in England: *R. v Heath* [1999] T.L.R. 689. Secondly, the accused cannot found on coercion when he has voluntarily incurred the *risk* of liability to be subjected to it. Thus, if the accused in *Trotter* had been indebted to drug dealers, his defence would likely have been impossible if he had maintained that he had delivered the heroin to avoid being seriously assaulted but had accepted, as the accused in *Heath* had done, that the drugs world was "heavy" and that "people collect their debts in one way". In such circumstances the accused foresees the risk that he may be required by his creditors' threats of violence to commit a crime. As it has been suggested: "Perhaps the practice of the drug dealers is so common in the drugs world that those venturing into it do know this." (see J.C. Smith at [2000] Crim. L.R. 111). However, a different view has been expressed in *R. v Z* [2003] 1 W.L.R. 1489 in which a question of law has been certified for consideration by the House of Lords.

Notice of a defence of coercion (though not of the intention to rely on such evidence for the purposes of mitigation) should be given to the Crown, any co-accused and the appropriate court in solemn proceedings in terms of s.78(2) of the Criminal Procedure (Scotland) Act 1995 not less than 10 clear days before the trial diet (in High Court cases) or (in sheriff court cases) at or before the first diet. Failure to give such notice renders the plea incompetent. In *Trotter* the sheriff rejected the plea as incompetent but the Appeal Court did not require to consider the soundness of that decision which was challenged on the basis that the procurator fiscal had received informal notice of the defence in discussions in chambers in presence of the sheriff.

Being concerned in. The concept of being concerned in the supplying of (or the making to another of an offer to supply) a controlled drug (in s.4(3)b) and (c) respectively) is a broad one. The use of it in the creation of a criminal offence initially gave rise to some difficulty since its scope was not immediately or easily definable. For the purposes of Scots law the authoritative meaning of the phrase, in the context of s.4(3)(b), was provided by Lord Hunter, with whom Lord Justice-Clerk Ross expressly concurred, in *Kerr v H.M. Advocate*, 1986 S.C.C.R. 81; 1986 J.C. 41) when his Lordship said (1986 S.C.C.R. at 87) in a passage which is regularly read to juries:

> [S]ection 4(3)(b) was purposely enacted in the widest terms and was intended to cover a great variety of activities both at the centre and also on the fringes of dealing in controlled drugs. It would, for example, in appropriate circumstances include the activities of financiers, couriers and other go-betweens, lookouts, advertisers, agents and many links in the chain of distribution. It would certainly ... include the activities of persons who take part in the breaking up of bulk, the adulteration and reduction of purity, the separation and division into deals and the weighing and packaging of deals.

In charges under s.4(3)(b) it has been doubted whether there is room for the doctrine, of concert to be applied (*Salmon v H.M. Advocate; Moore v H.M. Advocate*, 1999 S.L.T. 169 at 182G–H and 187H; *H.M. Advocate v Hamill*, 1998 S.L.T. 1260 (Lord Marnoch)) although the point has not been finally determined (*cf. Farr, supra*).

It is irrelevant that the supply of drugs has been completed by the time the accused becomes concerned: demanding money for controlled drugs supplied by the accused's father a fortnight earlier is a contravention of s.4(3)(b) (*Douglas v Boyd*, 1996 S.L.T. 401; 1996 S.C.C.R. 44).

Defences

The offences specified in subsections (2) and (3) are stated as being subject to s.28 which contains specific provision for a defence of ignorance which the accused bears the onus of proving. In *Tudhope v McKee*, 1988 S.L.T. 153, Lord Justice-Clerk Ross described the offence under s.4(3)(b) as one of "strict liability subject only to the defence afforded by s.28 of the Act". This opinion, though not expressed by the other members of the court, has been taken to be accurate (see R.A.A. McCall Smith and D. Sheldon, *Scots Criminal Law* (2nd ed.), p.214) although in *Salmon and Moore, supra* at 178L Lord Justice-General Rodger drew attention to the ambiguous nature of the Lord Justice-Clerk's description. In particular, the reference to "only" is mistaken since s.28(4) expressly preserves any defence which it is open to an accused to raise apart from s.28. The correct view now is, as *Salmon and Moore* makes plain, that the Crown does not have to prove that the accused knew that the subject matter of the supply, or offer, or act of being concerned in, was a controlled drug. It does not mean that the Crown need prove nothing more than that as a matter of fact, the accused was involved in a transaction involving a controlled drug in order to shift the onus to the accused to prove ignorance of what he was involved in. The appropriate approach to s.28 defences is dealt with *infra*.

Attempt and incitement

While s.19 provides for Scotland that it is an offence for a person to attempt to commit an offence under s.4(2) and (3) or to incite another to commit such an offence, it would be highly unusual for a charge to be brought of attempting to be concerned in production, or supply or the making of an offer. The width of an offence of being concerned in is such as to include attempts. It is, however, possible that A could be charged with inciting B to commit any of the offences in subss.(2) and (3).

Restriction of Possession of Controlled Drugs

5. —(1) Subject to any regulations under section 7 of this Act for the time being in force, it shall not be lawful for a person to have a controlled drug in his possession.

(2) Subject to section 28 of this Act and to subsection (4) below, it is an offence for a person to have a controlled drug in his possession in contravention of subsection (1) above.

(3) Subject to section 28 of this Act, it is an offence for a person to have a controlled drug in his possession, whether lawfully or not, with intent to supply it to another in contravention of section 4(1) of this Act.

(4) In any proceedings for an offence under subsection (2) above in which

it is proved that the accused had a controlled drug in his possession, it shall be a defence for him to prove—

    (a) that, knowing or suspecting it to be a controlled drug, he took possession of it for the purpose of preventing another from committing or continuing to commit an offence in connection with that drug and that as soon as possible after taking possession of it he took all such steps as were reasonably open to him to destroy the drug or to deliver it into the custody of a person lawfully entitled to take custody of it; or

    (b) that, knowing or suspecting it to be a controlled drug, he took possession of it for the purpose of delivering it into the custody of a person lawfully entitled to take custody of it and that as soon as possible after taking possession of it he took all such steps as were reasonably open to him to deliver it into the custody of such a person.

    (5) Subsection (4) above shall apply in the case of proceedings for an offence under section 19(1) of this Act consisting of an attempt to commit an offence under subsection (2) above as it applies in the case of proceedings for an offence under subsection (2), subject to the following modifications, that is to say—

    (a) for the references to the accused having in his possession, and to his taking possession of, a controlled drug there shall be substituted respectively references to his attempting to get, and to his attempting to take, possession of such a drug; and

    (b) in paragraphs (a) and (b) the words from "and that as soon as possible" onwards shall be omitted.

    (6) Nothing in subsection (4) or (5) above shall prejudice any defence which it is open to a person charged with an offence under this section to raise apart from that subsection.

GENERAL NOTE

This provision is likely to be most commonly encountered in practice, especially in summary proceedings. All possession is unlawful save where under s.7 regulations have been made to render possession lawful. This has been done by the Misuse of Drugs Regulations 1985 (SI 1985/2066), paras 10 and 11 (see *infra*).

Two specific offences are created by this section. First, unlawful possession of any controlled drug is an offence under s.5(2) and, secondly, irrespective of the lawfulness of the possession, s.5(3) creates the offence of possession of a controlled drug with the specific intention of supplying it to another person. There are also further offences in relation to possession in s.19, namely: (i) attempted unlawful possession; (ii) attempted possession with intent to supply (see *Docherty v Brown*, 1996 S.L.T. 325; 1996 S.C.C.R. 136 which held that impossibility is no defence to such a charge); (iii) incitement of another person to possess a controlled drug unlawfully; and (iv) incitement of another to possess a controlled drug with intent.

The last two offences also include an attempt at incitement. It is suggested that this provision forecloses any further regression in liability so that it would not be possible to charge A with inciting B to (or attempt to) incite C to supply (or attempt to supply) a controlled drug to D.

Since the offence under s.5(2) is premised on the unlawfulness of the possession and since persons can be exempted from the operation of subs.(1) by regulations made under s.7 (see notes to s.4, *supra*), s.5(4) creates two specific defences which it is for the accused to prove (on a balance of probabilities, but without the necessity for corroboration: see *King v Lees*, 1993 S.L.T. 1184 at 1187F). The accused must be acquitted if he can prove that his possession of the controlled drug was acquired for the (sole) purpose of preventing crime and that he took all steps reasonably open to him to destroy the drug or to hand it in to a person lawfully entitled to take custody of it such as a police constable. This is an exacting requirement: if the accused takes nearly all reasonable steps his defence must fail. If the step not taken by him was one which did not occur to him but would occur to a reasonable man then the accused must be convicted. The second defence does not require the acquiring of possession to be for the purpose of preventing crime but rather for the purpose of delivering the drug to the relevant authority. These defences are, *mutatis mutandis*, available in a charge of attempting to possess (see s.5(5)).

That the defence in s.5(4)(a) is (understandably) exacting is demonstrated by the decision of the Court of Appeal (Criminal Division) in *R. v Murphy* [2003] 1 Cr.App.R. 276. The defendant found a block of herbal cannabis in the glove compartment of his fiancee's car and believing it to be his father's drugs and not wanting them to remain in a car for which he had responsibility (especially since he had a previous conviction under s.5(3) of the 1971 Act in respect of cannabis), he buried the cannabis in a hole in the gravel of the car park at a prison where he was intending to visit a friend. The prosecution accepted (because they could not dispute: see 280) that the defendant had no intention of later retrieving the cannabis and that ultimately the forces of nature would destroy the cannabis. The trial judge refused to leave the defence under s.5(4)(a) to the jury. The defendant's appeal was dismissed. Longmore L.J. stated (at 279): "It cannot be sufficient ... that in the end the forces of nature might or would destroy a quantity of drugs. ... The statute envisages that if there is to be a defence it is for the defendant to show that he took all such steps as were reasonably open to him to destroy the drug and envisages that the act of destruction must be his." Furthermore, destruction required a great deal more finality about it than what the defendant did because the court agreed with the prosecution's argument that "the mere fact that it might, in the circumstances of a particular case, be difficult or impossible to show that a particular defendant ... had taken all reasonable steps to destroy the drugs would not mean that that of itself could give the defendant a defence". (However, the court criticised the Crown for insisting in the prosecution, quashed the defendant's conditional discharge for two years and imposed an absolute discharge.)

ECHR compatibility of reverse onus provision

The imposition of a burden on accused persons under s.5(4) could arguably be incompatible with Article 6. The gravamen of the offence is unlawful possession. While it can be accepted that the only person likely to know why he had possession is the accused, it does not follow that he should be convicted even where the jury entertain a reasonable doubt as to the purpose of his possession. Such an approach is in conformity with the reasoning of the Divisional Court in *Sheldrake v DPP* [2003] 1 W.L.R. 1629 where the rationale of the House of Lords' decision in *R. v Lambert* [2002] 2 A.C. 545 was explained (see also *Attorney-General's Reference (No.4 of 2002)* [2003] T.L.R. 189). It might therefore be necessary to read s.5(4) down so as to impose an evidential burden only on the accused. At present an accused's possession is in effect presumed to be unlawful, under s.5(1), until he shows that it was for one or other of the purposes in s.5(4). On the other hand, it might be argued that it would impose an undue, if not impossible, burden on the Crown to exclude such purposes. That seems to have been the Crown's problem in *Murphy* but that, rather ironically, is precisely why the Court of Appeal regarded the offence as being of the "utmost technicality".

Possession

The traditional Scots law approach to possession was derived from the decision of the High Court in *Black v H.M. Advocate*, 1974 J.C. 43; 1974 S.L.T. 247 which was concerned with possession under s.4(1) of the Explosive Substances Act 1883 (46 & 47 Vict., c.3). Adapting *Black's* ratio, the courts required for possession under the controlled drugs legislation that the accused be proved to have had both knowledge of the existence or presence of a thing which turned out to be a controlled drug and control over it (see *Mingay v Mackinnon*, 1980 J.C. 33 at 35). Subject to the qualifications which apply as a result of the introduction of the statutory defences in s.28(2) and (3) (see *infra*) and the possible relaxation in the meaning applied by the courts to the concept of "control", that remains the requirements of Scots law (see, *e.g.* *Hughes v Guild*, 1990 S.L.T. 715 at 717K).

It is not necessary for the Crown to prove that the accused knew that he was in possession of a controlled drug (*Salmon v H.M. Advocate*; *Moore v H.M. Advocate*, 1999 S.L.T. 169) far less that he knew that it was the particular drug libelled (*R. v Leeson* [2000] 1 Cr.App.R. 233; [1999] T.L.R. 732).

Premises in multiple occupation

Difficulties arise because in many cases more than one person has access to the place where the controlled drug is found (see, *e.g.* *Lustman v Stewart*, 1971 S.L.T. (Notes) 58). The High Court considered this problem in *Hughes v Guild*, 1990 S.L.T. 715 where the court relied on the statutory extension of "possession" in s.37(3) (what a person has in his possession shall be taken to include any thing subject to his control which is in the custody of another) and stated:

"Section 37(3) ... tells us that the things which a person has in his possession shall be taken to include anything subject to his control which is in the custody of another. That extends the meaning of possession, but it also shows that control is necessary for there to be possession and that the power to dispose of the article is the essence of control. Mere knowledge of the presence is not enough, because the person must be in a position to exercise practical control over it in some way."

Thus where the persons charged are the only occupiers and the controlled drug is open to view in the flat, if knowledge is established, "it is a relatively short step to say that there was control also". *Hughes* might suggest that the Crown should always charge all occupiers in order to establish joint possession against all of them. For a discussion of joint possession, see P.W. Ferguson, "Joint Possession of Controlled Drugs", 1990 S.L.T. (News) 233 and R.S. Shiels, "Controlled Drugs and Premises of Multiple Occupancy" [1998] Crim.L.R. 404.

Minute quantities

Possession of minute quantities is no less criminal. The test applied by the Scottish courts is whether the controlled drug is capable of identification in a suitable manner (*Keane v Gallacher*, 1980 J.C. 77; 1980 S.L.T. 144). This approach has been criticised (see *Stair Memorial Encyclopaedia of the Laws of Scotland*, Vol.14, para.1240) because, for example, once a substance has been used in a room, it is possible that minute traces might remain in the dust in the room indefinitely. In such circumstances it is impossible for the occupier ever to abandon possession, more especially since one does not cease to be in possession merely because through passage of time one has forgotten about the drug (*Gill v Lockhart*, 1988 S.L.T. 189; *R. v Martindale* [1986] 1 W.L.R. 1042).

Restriction of Cultivation of Cannabis Plant

6. —(1) Subject to any regulations under section 7 of this Act for time being in force, it shall not be lawful for a person to cultivate any plant of the genus Cannabis.

(2) Subject to section 28 of this Act, it is an offence to cultivate any such plant in contravention of subsection (1) above.

GENERAL NOTE

It is for the accused to prove on balance of probabilities (but without the necessity for corroboration) that he did not know nor suspect nor have reason to suspect that the plant which he was cultivating was a species of the *genus cannabis* (see *R. v Champ* [1981] 73 Cr.App.R. 367). Cannabis cultivation can be licensed by the Secretary of State and where this is done, provided the conditions of the licence are adhered to, the cultivation is rendered lawful (see Misuse of Drugs Regulations 1985 (SI 1985/2066), para.12).

...

Miscellaneous Offences Involving Controlled Drugs, etc.

Occupiers etc. of Premises to be Punishable for Permitting Certain Activities to Take Place There

8. A person commits an offence if, being the occupier or concerned in the management of any premises, he knowingly permits or suffers any of the following activities to take place on those premises, that is to say—
   (a) producing or attempting to produce a controlled drug in contravention of section 4(1) of this Act;
   (b) supplying or attempting to supply a controlled drug to another in contravention of section 4(1) of this Act, or offering to supply a controlled drug to another in contravention of section 4(1);
   (c) preparing opium for smoking;
   (d) smoking cannabis, cannabis resin or prepared opium.

AMENDMENT

Subs.(d) prospectively amended by the Criminal Justice and Police Act 2001 (c.16), s.38.

GENERAL NOTE

This set of offences is not subject to the defences set out in s.28 because each of the offences in paras (a) to (d) requires the Crown to prove knowledge on the part of the accused as to the proscribed activities which he permits or suffers to take place on his premises. All that the Crown need prove is the activity and there is no requirement that the accused be proved to have known which controlled drug was involved in the charge (*R. v Bett* [1998] T.L.R. 673).

In respect of a charge of contravention of s.8(b) the Court of Appeal (Criminal Division) has held that a belief by the accused that he had taken reasonable steps to prevent the commission of the offence did not afford any defence: it was for the jury to judge the accused's conduct (*R. v Brock* [2000] T.L.R. 906). What the Crown has to establish on a charge of "permitting" is (i) either actual knowledge or wilful blindness (by closing one's eyes to the obvious) that the offence is being committed and (ii) unwillingness to prevent the offence, which can be inferred from a failure to take reasonable steps, which are readily available, to prevent it. In *Brock* the court also held that the jury should be directed, where appropriate, that in assessing what steps an accused should reasonably have taken to prevent the offence, regard should be had to the accused's level of knowledge of the dealing (and, similarly, the production of the drug, or preparation or smoking of the drug).

This decision has been criticised on apparently somewhat sociological grounds (see N. Padfield, "Managing premises used for the supply of heroin" (2001) 151 N.L.J. 507) but accords with the well settled meaning of the word "permit": the law sets the standard of what steps were reasonable to prevent the use but the accused's conduct is judged subjectively by reference to what circumstances of use he was aware of, including any to which he turned a blind eye: see J.C. Smith, [2001] Crim.L.R. 320.

Prohibition of Certain Activities etc. Relating to Opium

9. Subject to section 28 of this Act, it is an offence for a person—
(a)   to smoke or otherwise use prepared opium; or
(b)   to frequent a place used for the purpose of opium smoking; or
(c)   to have in his possession—
   (i)   any pipes or other utensils made or adapted for use in connection with the smoking of opium, being pipes or utensils which have been used by him or with his knowledge and permission in that connection or which he intends to use or permit others to use in that connection; or
   (ii)   any utensils which have been used by him or with his knowledge and permission in connection with the preparation of opium for smoking.

GENERAL NOTE

The onus is on the accused to prove on the balance of probabilities (but without the need for corroboration) that he did not know nor suspect nor have reason to suspect that the substance in question was prepared opium (*i.e.* opium prepared for smoking and any residue after it has been smoked: s.37(1)).

Prohibition of Supply etc. of Articles for Administering Preparing Controlled Drugs

9A. — (1) A person who supplies or offers to supply any article which may be used or adapted to be used (whether by itself or in combination with another article or other articles) in the administration by any person of a controlled drug to himself or another, believing that the article (or the article as adapted) is to be so used in circumstances where the administration is unlawful, is guilty of an offence.

(2) It is not an offence under subsection (1) above to supply or offer to supply a hypodermic syringe, or any part of one.

(3) A person who supplies or offers to supply any article which may be used to prepare a controlled drug for administration by any person to himself or another believing that the article is to be so used in circumstances where the administration is unlawful is guilty of an offence.

(4) For the purposes of this section, any administration of a controlled drug is unlawful except—

(a) the administration by any person of a controlled drug to another in circumstances where the administration of the drug is not unlawful under section 4(1) of this Act; or

(b) the administration by any person of a controlled drug to himself in circumstances where having the controlled drug in his possession is not unlawful under section 5(1) of this Act.

(5) In this section, references to administration by any person of a controlled drug to himself include a reference to his administering it to himself with the assistance of another.

AMENDMENT

Section 9A inserted by the Drug Trafficking Offences Act 1986 (c.32), s.34.

GENERAL NOTE

The essence of the offences created by subss.(1) and (3) is that the administration of the controlled drug (either to another or to himself with the assistance of another: s.9A(5)) is that the administration must be unlawful. All administration of a controlled drug for the purposes of s.9A is unlawful except as provided for in ss.4(1) or 5(1).

In England it has been stated that "there is no offence under the Misuse of Drugs Act 1971, or other statute, or at common law, of injecting oneself with a prohibited drug" (*R. v Dias* [2002] 2 Cr.App.R. 5 at para.21). The same, it is submitted, is true for Scots law. However, this provision comes very close to making self-injection an offence. Section 9A(4) and (5) together provide that administration of a controlled drug to oneself with another person's assistance is unlawful and s.9A(1) makes it an offence for a person to supply any article (other than a hypodermic syringe or any part of one: s.9A(2)) to another where that article may be used or adapted to be used (alone or in combination with other articles) in the administration by himself, or by that other person, of a controlled drug to himself. Thus, if A, being desirous of injecting himself with heroin, gave B a tourniquet which B then applied to A's arm to raise the vein in A's arm to allow A to inject himself, A and B would be guilty of the offence in s.9A(1). Moreover, in England it has been held that where death results—even where A has not supplied the tourniquet—B is guilty, as a principal, of both manslaughter and maliciously administering a noxious thing contrary to s.23 of the Offences Against the Person Act 1861 (see *R. v Rogers* [2003] 1 W.L.R. 1374). The same would apply in Scots law in respect of culpable homicide. For an interesting discussion of *Dias* and related cases, see Professor J.R. Spencer, "Furnishing someone with the means by which they kill themselves" (2002) Archbold News, (Issue 5) at 6–8.

  . . .

Power to Direct Special Precautions for Safe Custody of Controlled Drugs to be Taken at Certain Premises

11. —(1) Without prejudice to any requirement imposed by regulations made in pursuance of section 10(2)(a) of this Act, the Secretary of State may by notice in writing served on the occupier of any premises on which controlled drugs are or are proposed to be kept give directions as to the taking of precautions or further precautions for the safe custody of any controlled drugs of a description specified in the notice which are kept on those premises.

(2) It is an offence to contravene any directions given under subsection (1) above.

GENERAL NOTE

Section 10(2)(a) empowers the Secretary of State (for the purposes of preventing the misuse of controlled drugs) to make regulations providing for the requiring of precautions to be taken for the safe custody of controlled drugs. Such regulations are intended to apply generally and are found in the Misuse of Drugs (Safe Custody) Regulations 1973 (SI 1973/798). However, s.11 empowers the Secretary of State to make provision for specific premises on which controlled drugs are or are proposed to be kept, by means of written notices served on the individual occupiers. If the directions in the notice are not adhered to, the person responsible (whether occupier or his servant) is guilty of an offence (subs.(2)). Since s.28 is not applied to s.11, it is suggested that notwithstanding the regulatory nature of the 1971 Act, the courts will require *mens rea* for guilt to be established under s.11(2), in the form of knowledge on the accused's part of the existence of the direction which is alleged to have been contravened.

...

Miscellaneous Offences and Powers

Miscellaneous Offences

18. —(1) It is an offence for a person to contravene any regulations made under this Act other than regulations made in pursuance of section 10(2)(h) or (i).

(2) It is an offence for a person to contravene a condition or other term of a licence issued under section 3 of this Act or of a licence or other authority issued under regulations made under this Act, not being a licence issued under regulations made in pursuance of section 10(2)(l).

(3) A person commits an offence if, in purported compliance with any obligation to give information to which he is subject under or by virtue of regulations made under this Act, he gives any information which he knows to be false in a material particular or recklessly gives any information which is so false.

(4) A person commits an offence if, for the purpose of obtaining, whether for himself or another, the issue or renewal of a licence or other authority under this Act or under any regulations made under this Act, he—

    (a) makes any statement or gives any information which he knows to be false in a material particular, or recklessly gives any information which is so false; or

    (b) produces or otherwise makes use of any book, record or other document which to his knowledge contains any statement or information which he knows to be false in a material particular.

Attempts etc. to Commit Offences

19. It is an offence for a person to attempt to commit an offence under any other provision of this Act or to incite or attempt to incite another to commit such an offence.

GENERAL NOTE

See notes to ss.4 and 5, *supra.*

Assisting in or Inducing Commission Outside United Kingdom of Offence Punishable Under a Corresponding Law

20. A person commits an offence if in the United Kingdom he assists in or induces the commission in any place outside the United Kingdom of an offence punishable under the provisions of a corresponding law in force in that place.

GENERAL NOTE

The Crown in order to succeed must adduce evidence to prove (i) that the offence which the accused assists or induces was committed outside the United Kingdom and (ii) that that offence was punishable at the material time under the law of that foreign country (the "corresponding law"). Thus, so far as (i) is concerned, if A assists in an offence which because of police intervention, does not take place (for example, the importation of a controlled drug into a foreign country) then A cannot be convicted under s.20 (see *R. v Panayi and Karte* [1987] Crim.L.R. 764). Provision is made in s.36 for proof of the corresponding law to be by means of a certificate which is held to be sufficient evidence of the matters stated in it (s.36(2)).

Section 28 is not applied to s.20 offences and accordingly the courts will require evidence from which it can be inferred that the accused knew that he was assisting in or inducing a crime against the law of the foreign place.

Offences By Corporations

21. Where any offence under this Act or Part II of the Criminal Justice (International Co-operation) Act 1990, committed by a body corporate is proved to have been committed with the consent or connivance of, or to be attributable to any neglect on the part of, any director, manager, secretary or other similar officer of the body corporate, or any person purporting to act in any such capacity, he as well as the body corporate shall be guilty of that offence and shall be liable to be proceeded against accordingly.

AMENDMENTS

Section 21 as amended by the Criminal Justice (International Co-operation) Act 1990 (c.5), s.23 and the Drug Trafficking Act 1994 (c.37), Sch.1.

Section 21 as amended by the Proceeds of Crime Act 2002 (c.29), Sch.12. Brought into force on February 24, 2003 by the Proceeds of Crime Act 2002 (Commencement No.4, Transitional Provisions and Savings) Order 2003 (SI 2003/120 (C.6)).

GENERAL NOTE

This provision does not provide that a body corporate can be liable for any offence specified in the 1971 Act but provides that, on the assumption that such liability is brought home to the body corporate, since corporations can only act through the "directing mind" of the corporation (or at least its management), the director, manager, secretary or other officer (or any person purporting to act in such capacity) can also be liable where the offence was committed with that officer's consent or connivance or can be attributable to his neglect. The expression "body corporate" is not defined but is likely to be restricted to companies incorporated under the Companies Acts.

...

Law Enforcement and Punishment of Offences

Powers to Search and Obtain Evidence

23. — (1) A constable or other person authorised in that behalf by a general or special order of the Secretary of State shall, for the purposes of the execution of this Act, have power to enter the premises of a person carrying on business as a producer or supplier of any controlled drugs and to demand the production of, and to inspect, any books or documents relating to dealings in any such drugs and to inspect any stocks of any such drugs.

(2) If a constable has reasonable grounds to suspect that any person is in possession of a controlled drug in contravention of this Act or of any regulations made thereunder, the constable may—

(a) search that person, and detain him for the purpose of searching him;

    (b)   search any vehicle or vessel in which the constable suspects that the drug may be found, and for that purpose require the person in control of the vehicle or vessel to stop it;

    (c)   seize and detain, for the purposes of proceedings under this Act, anything found in the course of the search which appears to the constable to be evidence of an offence under this Act.

In this subsection "vessel" includes a hovercraft within the meaning of the Hovercraft Act, 1968; and nothing in this subsection shall prejudice any power of search or any power to seize or detain property which is exercisable by a constable apart from this subsection.

    (3) If a justice of the peace, a magistrate or a sheriff is satisfied by information on oath, that there is reasonable ground for suspecting—

    (a)   that any controlled drugs are, in contravention of this Act or of any regulations made thereunder, in the possession of a person on any premises; or

    (b)   that a document directly or indirectly relating to, or connected with, a transaction or dealing which was, or an intended transaction or dealing which would if carried out be, an offence under this Act, or in the case of a transaction or dealing carried out or intended to be carried out in a place outside the United Kingdom, an offence against the provisions of a corresponding law in force in that place, is in the possession of a person on any premises,

he may grant a warrant authorising any constable acting for the police area in which the premises are situated at any time or times within one month from the date of the warrant, to enter, if need be by force, the premises named in-the warrant, and to search the premises and any persons found therein and, if there is reasonable ground for suspecting that an offence under this Act has been committed in relation to any controlled drugs found on the premises or in the possession of any such persons, or that a document so found is such a document as is mentioned in paragraph (b) above, to seize and detain those drugs or that document, as the case may be.

    (3A) The powers conferred by subsection (1) above shall be exercisable also for the purposes of the execution of Part II of the Criminal Justice (International Co-operation) Act, 1990 and subsection (3) above (excluding paragraph (a)) shall apply also to offences under section 12 or 13 of that Act of 1990, taking references in those provisions to controlled drugs as references to scheduled substances within the meaning of that Part.

    (4) A person commits an offence if he—

    (a)   intentionally obstructs a person in the exercise of his powers under this section; or

    (b)   conceals from a person acting in the exercise of his powers under subsection (1) above any such books, documents, stocks or drugs as are mentioned in that subsection; or

    (c)   without reasonable excuse (proof of which shall lie on him) fails to produce any such books or documents as are so mentioned where their production is demanded by a person in the exercise of his powers under that subsection.

AMENDMENTS

Section 23(3A) inserted by the Criminal Justice (International Co-operation) Act 1990 (c.5), s.23(4).

Section 23(3A) as amended by the Drug Trafficking Act 1994 (c.37), Sch.1, para.4. Also amended by Proceeds of Crime Act 2002 (c.29), Sch.12. Brought into force on February 24, 2003 by the Proceeds of Crime Act 2002 (Commencement No.4, Transitional Provisions and Savings) Order 2003 (SI 2003/120 (C.6)).

GENERAL NOTE

The offence set out in s.23(4)(a) cannot be committed recklessly or negligently, far less accidentally. The powers the discharge of which are obstructed are set out in subss.(2) and (3) (see *Annan v McIntosh*, 1993 S.C.C.R. 938). "Obstruction" has been described as being either actual physical restraint or hindrance or in a figurative sense the doing of anything which is "done with intention to hinder officers in the discharge of their duty" (*Carmichael v Brannan*, 1986 S.L.T. 5 at 10C–D, *per* Lord Cameron). The commonly encountered form of obstruction is where A swallows a substance or thing on seeing police officers approach him (*e.g. Vannet v Taylor*, 1998 S.L.T. 1436).

Power of Arrest

24. —(1) A constable may arrest without warrant a person who has committed, or whom the constable, with reasonable cause, suspects to have committed, an offence under this Act, if—
 (a) he, with reasonable cause, believes that that person will abscond unless arrested; or
 (b) the name and address of that person are unknown to, and cannot be ascertained by, him; or
 (c) he is not satisfied that a name and address furnished by that person as his name and address are true.
 (2) This section shall not prejudice any power of arrest conferred by law apart from this section.

GENERAL NOTE

The power to arrest without warrant is personal to the constable in so far as it is exercised by the constable on the ground of his reasonable suspicion that the person has committed—not will commit—an offence under the 1971 Act (see *Woodward v Chief Constable, Fife Constabulary*, 1998 S.L.T. 1342).

The decision in *Woodward* was taken in the Outer House in an action of reparation for unlawful detention but was based on the House of Lords' decision in a Northern Irish appeal (*O'Hara v Chief Constable of the Royal Ulster Constabulary* [1997] A.C. 286). Neither *Woodward* nor *O'Hara* was cited to the Appeal Court in *Houston v Carnegie*, 2000 S.L.T. 333; 1999 S.C.C.R. 605 which was concerned with s.14(1) of the Criminal Procedure (Scotland) Act 1995. That provision enables a constable to detain a person where the constable has reasonable grounds for suspecting that a person has committed or is committing an offence punishable by imprisonment.

Houston is irreconcilable with *Woodward* and *O'Hara*. In *Houston* the sheriff repelled an objection to the admissibility of evidence obtained following detention of the accused on the ground that while the police officer had not applied his own mind to whether he had reasonable grounds for suspecting the accused of an offence and had merely detained the accused on a superior officer's orders, there were reasonable grounds in fact for the police officer to suspect the accused. Lord Prosser stated that the appropriate test under s.14(1) was an objective one and that where someone was detained by a constable who had not considered whether objectively available grounds for suspicion satisfied him that there were grounds for suspecting the accused, the detention was nonetheless lawful because reasonable grounds did exist, albeit that they were not the basis on which the constable acted (2000 S.L.T. 333 at 335C–D).

It should be noted that Art.5(1) of the European Convention on Human Rights requires that no one shall be deprived of his liberty save in the following circumstances, *inter alia*, "(c) the lawful arrest or detention of a person effected for the purpose of bringing him before the competent legal authority on reasonable suspicion of having committed an offence". The European Court has held that the approach of the domestic courts in *O'Hara* to the standard of suspicion required by Art.5(1)(c) had been satisfied because it had not "removed the accountability of the police for arbitrary arrest or conferred on the police any impunity with regard to arrests": see *O'Hara v United Kingdom* (Application No. 37555/97), Judgment of October 16, 2001 (at para.44). Thus, while the decision in *Houston* is open to criticism as being inconsistent with the House of Lords' approach in *O'Hara* to the personal nature of the power of detention and arrest in the relevant statutory provisions, it does not involve a violation of Art.5(1)(c).

In *McDonald v Procurator Fiscal, Dundee*, unreported, November 8, 2001, the Crown's submission based on *Houston v Carnegie* that a police officer's reasonable belief fell to be tested on an "objective" basis, was sustained by the High Court. However, as there was no dispute that the police officer had honestly believed that the accused had committed a breach of the peace, this decision does not add to or detract from the requirement which *Houston v Carnegie* disavows, that the police officer must himself entertain the suspicion and not merely exercise his powers on the basis of a suspicion formed by another.

Prosecution and Punishment of Offences

25. — (1) Schedule 4 to this Act shall have effect, in accordance with subsection (2) below, with respect to the way in which offences under this Act are punishable on conviction.

(2) In relation to an offence under a provision of this Act specified in the first column of the Schedule (the general nature of the offence being described in the second column)—

(a) the third column shows whether the offence is punishable on summary conviction or on indictment or in either way;

(b) the fourth, fifth and sixth column show respectively the punishments which may be imposed on a person convicted of the offence in the way specified in relation thereto in the third column (that is to say, summarily or on indictment) according to whether the controlled drug in relation to which the offence was committed was a Class A drug, a Class B drug or a Class C drug; and

(c) the seventh column shows the punishments which may be imposed on a person convicted of the offence in the way specified in relation thereto in the third column (that is to say, summarily or on indictment), whether or not the offence was committed in relation to a controlled drug and, if it was so committed, irrespective of whether the drug was a Class A drug, a Class B drug or a Class C drug;and in the fourth, fifth, sixth and seventh columns a reference to a period gives the maximum term of imprisonment and a reference to a sum of money the maximum fine.

(3) An offence under section 19 of this Act shall be punishable on summary conviction, on indictment or in either way according to whether, under Schedule 4 to this Act, the substantive offence is punishable on summary conviction, on indictment or in either way; and the punishments which may be imposed on a person convicted of an offence under that section are the same as those which, under that Schedule, may be imposed on a person convicted of the substantive offence.

In this subsection "the substantive offence" means the offence under this Act to which the attempt or, as the case may be, the incitement or attempted incitement mentioned in section 19 was directed.

(5) Notwithstanding anything in section 136, Criminal Procedure (Scotland) Act 1995, (limitations of time for proceedings in statutory offences) summary proceedings for an offence under this Act may be commenced at any time within twelve months from the time when the offence was committed, and subsection (3) of the said section 136 shall apply for the purposes of this subsection as it applies for the purposes of that section.

GENERAL NOTE

The High Court has held that s.25(5) directs that the six month time limit provided for in s.136(1) of the Criminal Procedure (Scotland) Act 1995 (which is the successor to s.23 of the Summary Jurisdiction (Scotland) Act 1954) should be disregarded in relation to offences under the Misuse of Drugs Act 1971 and that nothing in s.136(1) affects the operation of s.25(5) in the case of offences which can be tried both summarily and on indictment: see *Gilday v Miller*, 2000 J.C. 133.

...

Miscellaneous and Supplementary Provisions

Proof of Lack of Knowledge etc. to be a Defence in Proceedings for Certain Offences

28. — (1) This section applies to offences under any of the following provisions of this Act, that is to say section 4(2) and (3), section 5(2) and (3), section 6(2) and section 9.

(2) Subject to subsection (3) below, in any proceedings for an offence to which this section applies it shall be a defence for the accused to prove that he neither knew of nor suspected nor had reason to suspect the existence of some fact alleged by the prosecution which it is necessary for the prosecution to prove if he is to be convicted of the offence charged.

(3) Where in any proceedings for an offence to which this section applies it is necessary, if the accused is to be convicted of the offence charged, for the prosecution to prove that some substance or product involved in the alleged offence was the controlled drug which the prosecution alleges it to have been, and it is proved that the substance or product in question was that controlled drug, the accused—

    (a) shall not be acquitted of the offence charged by reason only of proving that he neither knew nor suspected nor had reason to suspect that the substance or product in question was the particular controlled drug alleged; but

    (b) shall be acquitted thereof—

        (i) if he proves that he neither believed nor suspected nor had reason to suspect that the substance or product in question was a controlled drug; or

        (ii) if he proves that he believed the substance or product in question to be a controlled drug, or a controlled drug of a description, such that, if it had in fact been that controlled drug or a controlled drug of that description, he would not at the material time have been committing any offence to which this section applies.

(4) Nothing in this section shall prejudice any defence which it is open to a person charged with an offence to which this section applies to raise apart from this section.

GENERAL NOTE

In the predecessor to the 1971 Act (the Drugs (Prevention of Misuse) Act 1964), there was no equivalent to s.28. This section was introduced by Parliament following the decision of the House of Lords in *Warner v Metropolitan Police Commissioner* [1969] 2 A.C. 256 in which the House had considered whether s.1 of the 1964 Act (relating to unlawful possession) was an absolute offence for which no *mens rea* was necessary. The speeches were not all to one effect but the judicial unease felt over the possibility of accused persons being imprisoned for many years for offences when they lacked any knowledge resulted in s.28 which was an attempt to balance the two concerns of making the controlled drugs regime practical for the purposes of enforcement and securing justice to individual accused in cases where the accused was justifiably unaware of the nature of his acts.

The effect of s.28(2) and (3) has been authoritatively considered by the High Court in *Salmon v H.M. Advocate; Moore v H.M. Advocate*, 1999 S.L.T. 169. In cases where the charge is based on possession the High Court held that where the drugs were in a container, it was sufficient for the Crown to prove that the accused knew that he had the container and that there was something in it. Even though the accused did not know that the contents were controlled drugs conviction would require to follow unless the accused could establish on a balance of probabilities that he did not know the contents were a controlled drug, nor suspected nor had reason to suspect that that was so. Where the charge involved an allegation that the accused was "concerned in" drugs activities, the Crown also had to establish knowledge in the sense that the accused knew that he was concerned in supplying something (or concerned in the production of something or the making of an offer to supply something) but he did not have to be proved to know what that thing was, far less that it was a controlled drug.

It follows that it is a misdirection for the jury to be told that the Crown must prove that the accused knew "the general character" of the thing which he had or was concerned with (*cf.*, *Sim v H.M. Advocate*, 1996 S.C.C.R. 77, criticised in *Salmon* at 176L) but as it is favourable to the accused it will not found an appeal on the basis of a miscarriage of justice.

In *Salmon* both Lord Justice-General Rodger and Lord Bonomy expressed doubt as to the scope which existed for the doctrine of concert to apply in cases of being concerned in the supply of controlled drugs (see 182G–H and 187H). It is, however, clear that the mental element necessary for an offence of art and part unlawful possession is the same as that for being involved as a principal. This is contrary to the traditional view that an accessory to a strict liability offence must be proved to know what he is an accomplice to but it has been explained by Sheriff Gordon as the possible result of the special nature of the offences set out in the 1971 Act (see commentary at 1998 S.C.C.R. 781E).

In *Duffin v H.M. Advocate*, 2000 J.C. 316 (at 318A, *per* L.J.-C. Cullen) it has been reiterated that it is doubtful what, if any, room there is for the application of the doctrine of concert to charges under s.4(3)(b).

Human Rights and Reverse Onus Provisions

Section 28 imposes a persuasive burden on the accused who may now, since the incorporation of the European Convention on Human Rights by virtue of the Scotland Act 1998 (c.46) and, more importantly, the Human Rights Act 1998 (c.42) (which came into force on October 2, 2000), be justified in challenging the provision as a violation of his rights under Art.6(2) of the European Convention. Article 6(2) provides: "Everyone charged with a criminal offence shall be presumed innocent until proved guilty according to law."

There is no decision of the European Court of Human Rights on the propriety of s.28 although the Court has recognised that presumptions of fact or law operate in every legal system and has stated, generally, that "[c]learly, the Convention does not prohibit such presumptions in principle. It does, however, require the Contracting States to remain within certain limits in this respect as regards criminal law." However, the Court proceeded to declare that the right to be presumed innocent is in particular intended to enshrine the fundamental principle of the rule of law and accordingly: "Article 6(2) does not therefore regard presumptions of fact or of law provided for in the criminal law with indifference. It requires States to confine them within reasonable limits which take into account the importance of what is at stake and maintain the rights of the defence" (*Salabiaku v France*, Series A No.141-A (1989); 13 E.H.R.R. 379 at para.28). Human rights jurisprudence therefore permits reverse onus provisions in the criminal law provided that they are strictly limited by reference to (1) whether what is at stake is important and (2) maintaining the accused's rights of defence (his implied right under Art.6 to an "equality of arms").

While there is no Scottish decision on this issue it is inevitable that the High Court shall follow the recent decision of the House of Lords in *R. v Lambert* [2001] 3 W.L.R. 206 where it was held that in order for s.28 to be compatible with Art.6(2) of the Convention it must be "read down" so as to impose only an evidential burden on the accused.

Interrelationship of s.28 with s.5(4) defences

The principal distinction between the defences set out in s.28, which impose an evidential burden only on the accused, and the two specific defences in s.5(4) (see *supra*) appears to be the accused's knowledge or suspicion that the "thing" is a controlled drug. It is not yet established that the s.5(4) defences can be "read down" to impose only an evidential burden but if they are not to be thus reinterpreted, the somewhat anomalous situation is conceivable that it will be less disadvantageous for the accused, in whose car is found a quantity of cannabis, to claim that he did not know or suspect what the article was than that, suspecting that it was drugs, his purpose was to destroy it or deliver it to the police.

...

Meaning of "Corresponding Law", and Evidence of Certain Matters by Certificate

36. — (1) In this Act the expression "corresponding law" means a law stated in a certificate purporting to be issued by or on behalf of the government of a country outside the United Kingdom to be a law providing for the control and regulation in that country of the production, supply, use, export and import of drugs and other substances in accordance with the provisions of the Single Convention on Narcotic Drugs signed at New York on 30th March, 1961, or a law providing for the control and regulation in that country of the production, supply, use, export and import of dangerous or otherwise harmful drugs in pursuance of any treaty, convention or other agreement or arrangement to which the government of that country and Her Majesty's Government in the United Kingdom are for the time being parties.

(2) A statement in any such certificate as aforesaid to the effect that any facts constitute an offence against the law mentioned in the certificate shall be sufficient evidence of the matters stated.

GENERAL NOTE

There is no provision for the accused to dispute the terms of the certificate but it is submitted that that does not exclude the right of the accused to lead evidence of foreign law to displace the evidential effect of the certificate. If the accused intends to dispute the certificate the only notice of that intention will be the inclusion of a relevant witness's name in the defence list of witnesses. It would, however, be preferable for provision to be made by amendment of the Act of Adjournal (Criminal Procedure Rules) 1996 (SI 1996/513) for the accused to be required to give notice of his intention before the trial by written intimation.

...

SCHEDULES

...

SCHEDULE 2

Controlled Drugs

Part I

Class A Drugs

(1) The following substances and products, namely:—
    (a) —

Acetorphine
Alfentanil
Allylprodine
Alphacetylmethadol
Alphameprodine
Alphamethadol
Alphamethadol
Alphaprodine
Anileridine
Benzethidine
Benzylmorphine
  (3-benzylmorphine)
Betacetylmethadol
Betameprodine
Betamethadol
Betaprodine
Bezitramide
Bufotenine
Cannabinol, except where contained
  in cannabis or cannabis resin
Cannabinol derivatives
Carfentanil
Clonitazene
Coca leaf
Cocaine
Desomorphine
Dextromoramide
Diamorphine
Diampromide
Diethylthiambutene
Difenoxin
  (1-(3-cyano-3,3-
  diphenylpropyl-4
  phenylpiperidine-4-
  carboxylic acid)
Lofentanil
Lysergamide
Lysergide and other *N*-alkyl
  derivatives of lysergamide
Mescaline

Dihydrocodeinone
O-carboxymethyloxime
Dihydromorphine
Dimenoxadole
Dimepheptanol
Dimethylthiambutene
Dimethylthiambutene
Dioxaphetyl butyrate
Diphenoxylate
Dipipanone
Drotebanol
  (3, 4-dimethoxy-17-methyl-
  morphinan-6B, 14-diol)
Ecgonine, and any derivative of
  ecgonine which is
  convertible to ecgonine or to
  cocaine
Ethylmethylthiambutene
Eticyclidine
Etonitazene
Etorphine
Etoxeridine
Etryptamine
Fentanyl
Furethidine
Hydrocordone
Hydromorphinol
Hydromorphone
Hydroxypethidine
Isomethadone
Ketobemidone
Levomethorpan
Levomoramide
Levophenacylmorphan
Levorphanol
Methadone
Methadyl acetate
Methyldesorphine
Methyldihydromorphine
  (6-methyldihydromorphine)

Metazocine
Morpheridine
Morphine
Morphine methobromide, morphine
N-oxide and other
    pentavelent nitrogen
    morphine derivatives
Myrophine
Nicomorphine
    (3,6-dinicotinoylmorphine)
Noracymethadol
Norlevorphanol
Normethadone
Normorphine
Norpipanone
Opium, whether raw, prepared or
    medicinal
Oxycodone
Oxymorphone
Pethidine
Phenadoxone
Phenampromide
Phenazocine
Phencyclidine
Phenomorphan
Phenoperidine
Piminodine
Piritramide
Poppy-straw and concentrate of
    poppy-straw
Proheptazine
Properidine
    (1-methyl-4-phenyl-

Metopon
    piperidine-4-
    carboxylic acid
    isopropylester
Psilocin
Racemetorphan
Racemoramide
Racemorphan
Rolicyclidine
Sufentanil
Tenocyclidine
Thebacon
Thebaine
Tilidate
Trimeperidene
4-Bromo-2,5-dimethoxy-
    methylphenethylamine
4-Cyano-2-dimethylamino-4,4-
    diphenylbutane
4-Cyano-1-methyl-4-
    phenylpiperidine
N,N-Diethyltryptamine
N,N-Dimethylphenethylamine
2,5-Dimethoxy-α, 4-
    dimethylphenethylamine
N-Hydroxy-tenamphetamine
1-Methyl-4-phenylpiperidine-4-
    carboxylic acid
2-Methyl-3-morpholino-1,1-
    diphenylpropanecarboxylic
    acid
4-Methyl-aminorex
4-Phenylpiperidine-4-carb
    acid ethyl ester

(b) any compounds (not being a compound for the time being specified in sub-paragraph (a) above) structurally derived from tryptamine or from a ring-hydroxy tryptamine by substitution at the nitrogen atom of the sidechain with one or more alkyl substituents but no other substituent;

(c) any compound (not being methoxyphenamine or a compound for the time being specified in sub-paragraph (a) above) structurally derived from phenethylamine, an N-alkylphenethylamine, α-methylphenethylamine, an N-alkyl-α-methylphenethylamine, α-ethylphenethyl amine, or an N-alkyl-α-ethylphenethylamine by substitution in the ring to any extent with alkyl, alkoxy, alkylenedioxy or halide substituents, whether or not further substituted in the ring by one or more other univalent substituents;

(d) any compound (not being a compound for the time being specified in sub-paragraph (a) above) structurally derived from fentanyl by modification in any of the following ways, that is to say,
  (i) by replacement of the phenyl portion of the phenethyl group by any heteromonocycle whether or not further substituted in the heterocycle;
  (ii) by substitution in the phenethyl group with alkyl, alkenyl, alkoxy, hydroxy, halogeno, haloalkyl, amino or nitro groups;
  (iii) by substitution in the piperidine ring with alkyl or alkenyl groups;
  (iv) by substitution in the aniline ring with alkyl, alkoxy, alkylenedioxy, halogeno or haloalkyl groups;
  (v) by substitution at the 4-position of the piperidine ring with any alkoxycarbonyl or alkoxyalkyl or acyloxy group;

  (vi) by replacement of the N-propionyl group by another acyl group;

 (e) any compound (not being a compound for the time being specified in sub-paragraph
   (a) above) structurally derived from pethidine by modification in any of the following ways, that is to say,

   (i) by replacement of the l-methyl group by an acyl, alkyl whether or not unsatu-
    rated, benzyl or phenethyl group, whether or not further substituted;

   (ii) by substitution in the piperidine ring with alkyl or alkenyl groups or with a pro-
    pano bridge, whether or not further substituted;

   (iii) by substitution in the 4-phenyl ring with alkyl, alkoxy, aryloxy, halogeno or ha-
    loalkyl groups;

   (iv) by replacement of the 4-ethoxycarbonyl by any other alkoxy-carbonyl or any
    alkoxyalkyl or acyloxy group;

   (v) by formation of an N-oxide or of a quaternary base.

 (2) Any stereoisomeric form of a substance for the time being specified in paragraph (1) above
not being dextromethorphan or dextrophan.

 (3) Any ester or ether of a substance for the time being specified in paragraph (1) or (2) above,
not being a substance for the time being specified in Part II of this schedule.

 (4) Any salt of a substance for the time being specified in any of paragraphs (1) to (3) above.

 (5) Any preparation or other product containing a substance or product for the time being
specified in any of paragraphs (1) to (4) above.

 (6) Any preparation designed for administration by injection which includes a substance or
product for the time being specified in any of paragraphs (1) to (3) of Part II of this Schedule.

Part II

Class B Drugs

 (1) The following substances and products, namely:—

  (a)

Acetyldihydrocodeine	Methylamphetamine
Amphetamine	Methylphenidate
Cannabis and cannabis	Methylphenobarbitone
resin	Nicocodine
Codeine	Nicodicodine (6-
Dihydrocodeine	nicotinoyldihydrocodeine)
Ethylmorphine	Norcodeine
(3-ethylmorphine)	Pentazocine
Glutethimide	Phenmetrazine
Lefetamine	Pholcodine
Macloqualone	Propiram.
Methaqualone	Zipeprol
Methcathione	

  (b) any 5,5 disubstituted barbituric acid.

 (2) Any stereoisomeric form of a substance for the time being specified in paragraph (1) of this
Part of this Schedule.

 (3) Any salt of a substance for the time being specified in paragraph (1) or (2) of this Part of
this Schedule.

 (4) Any preparation or other product containing a substance or product for the time being
specified in any of paragraphs (1) to (3) of this Part of this Schedule, not being a preparation
falling within paragraph (6) of Part I of this Schedule.

Part III

Class C Drugs

 (1) The following substances, namely:—

 (a)

Alprazolam	Bromazepam
Aminorex	Buprenorphine
Benzphetamine	Brotizolan
Camazepam	Loprazolam
Cathine	Lorazepam
Cathinone	Lormetazepam
Chlorodiazepoxide	Mazindol
Chlorophentermine	Medazepam
Clobazam	Mefenorex
Clonazepam	Mephentermine
Clorazepic acid	Meprobamate
Clotiazepam	Mesocarb
Cloxazolam	Methylprylone
Delorazepam	Midazolam
Dextropropoxyphene	Nimetazepam
Diazepam	Nitrazepam
Diethylpropion	Nordazepam
Estazolam	Oxazepam
Ethclorvynol	Oxazolam
Ethinamate	Pemoline
Ethyl loflazepate	Phendimetrazine
Fencamfamin	Phentermine
Fenethylline	Pinazepam
Fenproporex	Pipradol
Fludiazepam	Prazepam
Flunitrazepam	Pyrovalerone
Flurazepam	Temazepam
Halazepam	Tetrazepam
Haloxazolam	Triazolam
Ketazolam	*N*-Ethylamphetamine

(2)   Any stereoisomeric form of a substance for the time being specified in paragraph (1) of this Part of this Schedule not being phenylpropanolamine.

(3)   Any salt of a substance for the time being specified in paragraph (1) or (2) of this Part of this Schedule.

(4)   Any preparation or other product containing a substance for the time being specified in any of paragraphs (1) to (3) of this Part of this Schedule.

(b)

Atamestane	Methenolone
Bolandiol	Methyltestosterone
Bolasterone	Metribolone
Bolazine	Mibolerone
Boldenone	Nandrolene
Bolenol	Norboletone
Bolmantalate	Norclosetebol
Calusterone	Norethandrolene
4-Chloromethandienone	Ovandrotone
Clostebol	Oxabolone
Drostanolone	Oxandrolone
Enestebol	Oxymesterone
Epitiostanol	Oxymetholone
Ethyloestrenol	Prasterone
Fluoxymesterone	Propetandrol
Formebolone	Quinbolone
Furazabol	Roxibolone
Mebolazine	Silandrone

Mepitiostane	Stanolone
Mesabolone	Stanozolol
Mestanolone	Stenbolone
Mesterolone	Testosterone
Methandienone	Thiomesterone
Methandriol	Trenbolone

(c) any compound (not being Trilostane or a compound for the time being specified in sub-paragraph (b) above) structurally derived from 17-hydroxyandrostan-3-one or from 17-hydroxyestran-3-one by modification in any of the following ways, that is to say,
   (i) by further substitution at position 17 by a methyl or ethyl group;
   (ii) by substitution to any extent at one or more of positions 1, 2, 4, 6, 7, 9, 11 or 16, but at no other position;
   (iii) by unsaturation in the carbocyclic ring system to any extent, provided that there are no more than two ethylenic bonds in any one carbocyclic ring;
   (iv) by fusion of ring A with a heterocyclic system;
(d) any substance which is an ester or ether (or, where more than one hydroxyl function is available, both an ester and an ether) of a substance specified in sub-paragraph (b) or described in sub-paragraph (c) above;
(e) Chorionic Gonadotrophin (HCG).
   Clenbuterol.
   Non-human chorionic gonadotrophin.
   Somatotropin.
   Somatrem.
   Somatropin.

PART IV

MEANING OF CERTAIN EXPRESSIONS USED IN THIS SCHEDULE

For the purposes of this Schedule the following expressions (which are not among those defined in Section 37(1) of this Act) have the meanings hereby assigned to them respectively, that is to say—

"cannabinol derivatives" means the following substances, except where contained in cannabis or cannabis resin, namely tetrahydro derivatives of cannabinol and 3-alkyl homologues of cannabinol or of its tetrahydro derivatives;

"coca leaf" means the leaf of any plant of the genus *Erythroxylon* from whose leaves cocaine can be extracted either directly or by chemical transformation;

"concentrate of poppy-straw" means the material produced when poppy-straw has entered into a process for the concentration of its alkaloids;

"medicinal opium" means raw opium which has undergone the process necessary to adapt it for medicinal use in accordance with the requirements of the British Pharmacopoeia, whether it is in the form of powder or is granulated or is in any other form, and whether it is or is not mixed with neutral substances;

"opium poppy" means the plant of the species *Papaver somniferum* L;

"poppy straw" means all parts, except the seeds, of the opium poppy, after mowing;

"raw opium" includes powdered or granulated opium but does not include medicinal opium.

AMENDMENTS

Part III as amended by the Misuse of Drugs Act 1971 (Modification, Order 1996 (SI 1996/1300) art.2(2)(a).

Part III, (4)(b)–(e) inserted by art.2(2)(b) of the above Order.

Sch.2 as amended by the Misuse of Drugs Act 1971 (Modification) Order 1998 (SI 1998/750) art.2(2) (effective May 1, 1998).

Part II, (1)(a) as amended by art.2(3) of the above Order.

Part III, (1)(a) as amended by art.2(4) of the above Order.

. . .

SCHEDULE 4

PROSECUTION AND PUNISHMENT OFFENCES

Section Creating Offence	General Nature of Offence	Mode of Prosecution	Punishment			
			Class A drug involved	Class B drug involved	Class C drug involved	General
Section 4(2)	Production, or being concerned in the production, of a controlled drug.	(a) Summary	12 months or the prescribed sum, or both.	12 months or the prescribed sum, or both.	3 months or £2,500, or both.	
		(b) On indictment	Life or a fine, or both.	14 years or a fine, or both.	5 years or a fine, or both.	
Section 4(3)	Supplying or offering to supply a controlled drug or being concerned in the doing of either activity by another.	(a) Summary	12 months or the prescribed sum, or both.	12 months or the prescribed sum,	3 months or £2,500, or both.	
		(b) On indictment	Life or a fine, or both.	14 years or a fine, or both.	5 years or a fine, or both.	
Section 5(2)	Having possession of a controlled drug.	(a) Summary	12 months or the prescribed sum, or both.	3 months or £2,500, or both.	3 months or £1,000, or both.	
		(b) On indictment	7 years or a fine or both.	5 years or a fine or both.	2 years or a fine or both.	
Section 5(3)	Having possession of a controlled drug with intent to supply it to another.	(a) Summary	12 months or the prescribed sum, or both.	12 months or the prescribed sum, or both.	3 months or £2,500, or both.	
		(b) On indictment	Life or a fine, or both.	14 years or a fine, or both.	5 years or a fine, or both.	
Section 6(2)	Cultivation of cannabis plant.	(a) Summary	—	—	—	12 months or the prescribed sum, or both.

Section Creating Offence	General Nature of Offence	Mode of Prosecution	Punishment			
			Class A drug involved	Class B drug involved	Class C drug involved	General
Section 8	Being the occupier, or concerned in the management, of premises and permitting or suffering certain activities to take place there.	(a) Summary	12 months or the prescribed sum, or both.	12 months or the prescribed sum, or both.	3 months or £2,500, or both.	—
		(b) On indictment	14 years or a fine, or both.	14 years or a fine, or both.	5 years or a fine, or both.	—
Section 9	Offences relating to opium.	(a) Summary	—	—	—	12 months or the prescribed sum, or both.
		(b) On indictment	—	—	—	14 years or a fine, or both.
Section 9A	Prohibition of supply etc. of articles for administering or preparing controlled drugs.	Summary	—	—	—	6 months or level 5 on the standard scale or both.
Section 11(2)	Contravention of directions relating to safe custody of controlled drug.	(a) Summary	—	—	—	6 months or the prescribed sum, or both.
		(b) On indictment	—	—	—	2 years or a fine or both.
Section 12(6)	Contravention of direction prohibiting practitioner etc. from possessing, supplying etc. controlled drugs.	(a) Summary	12 months or the prescribed sum, or both.	12 months or the prescribed sum, or both.	3 months or £2,500, or both.	—

Section Creating Offence	General Nature of Offence	Mode of Prosecution	Punishment			
			Class A drug involved	Class B drug involved	Class C drug involved	General
		(b) On indictment	14 years or a fine, or both.	5 years or a fine, or both.	5 years or a fine, or both.	
Section 13(3)	Contravention of direction prohibiting practitioner etc. from prescribing, supplying etc. controlled drugs.	*(a)* Summary	12 months or the prescribed sum, or both.	12 months or the prescribed sum, or both.	3 months or £2,500, or both.	
		(b) On indictment	14 years or a fine, or both.	14 years or a fine, or both.	5 years or a fine, or both.	
Section 17(3)	Failure to comply with notice requiring information relating to prescribing, supply etc. of drugs.	Summary	—	—	—	Level 3 on the standard scale.
Section 17(4)	Giving false information in purported compliance with notice requiring information relating to prescribing, supplying etc. of drugs.	*(a)* Summary	—	—	—	6 months or the prescribed sum or both.
		(b) On indictment	—	—	—	2 years or a fine or both.
Section 18(1)	Contravention of regulations (other than regulations relating to addicts)	*(a)* Summary	—	—	—	6 months or the prescribed sum or both.
		(b) On indictment	—	—	—	2 years or a fine or both.

Section Creating Offence	General Nature of Offence	Mode of Prosecution	Punishment			
			Class A drug involved	Class B drug involved	Class C drug involved	General
Section 18(2)	Contravention of terms of licence or other authority (other than regulations relating to addicts).	(a) Summary	—	—	—	6 months or the prescribed sum or both.
		(b) On indictment	—	—	—	2 years or a fine or both.
Section 18(3)	Giving false information in purported compliance with obligation to give information imposed under or by virtue of regulations.	(a) Summary	—	—	—	6 months or the prescribed sum or both.
		(b) On indictment	—	—	—	2 years or a fine or both.
Section 18(4)	Giving false information, or producing document etc. containing false statement etc., for purposes of obtaining issue or renewal of a licence or other authority.	(a) Summary	—	—	—	6 months or the prescribed sum or both.
		(b) On indictment	—	—	—	2 years or a fine or both.
Section 20	Assisting in or inducing commission outside United Kingdom of an offence punishable under a corresponding law.	(a) Summary	—	—	—	12 months or the prescribed sum or both.

Section Creating Offence	General Nature of Offence	Mode of Prosecution	Punishment			
			Class A drug involved	Class B drug involved	Class C drug involved	General
		(b) On indictment	—	—	—	14 years or a fine or both.
Section 23(4)	Obstructing exercise of powers of search etc. or concealing books, drugs etc.	(a) Summary	—	—	—	6 months or the prescribed sum or both.
		(b) On indictment	—	—	—	2 years or a fine or both.

33

CUSTOMS AND EXCISE MANAGEMENT ACT 1979

(1979 C.2)

An Act to consolidate the enactments relating to the collection and management of the revenues of customs and excise and in some cases to other matters in relation to which the Commissioners of Customs and Excise for the time being perform functions, with amendments to give effect to recommendations of the Law Commission and the Scottish Law Commission.

[22nd February 1979]

GENERAL NOTE AND INTRODUCTION

The Customs and Excise Management Act 1979 contains the offences which are prosecuted in respect of the prohibition contained in s.3 of the Misuse of Drugs Act 1971 (c.38) in relation to controlled drugs, as well as in respect of the evasion of excise duties. While the 1979 Act has not been much considered in the Scottish courts, it has been the subject of judicial analysis in England as has the predecessor to the 1979 Act, namely the Customs and Excise Act 1952 (c.44) which so far as relevant, was in identical terms. The important provisions are ss.50, 68 and 170.

Preliminary

Interpretation

1. —(1) In this Act, unless the context otherwise requires—
"aerodrome" means any area of land or water designed, equipped, set apart of commonly used for affording facilities for the landing and departure of aircraft;
"approved route" ...
"approved wharf" has the meaning given by section 20A below;
"armed forces" means the Royal Navy, the Royal Marines, the regular army and the regular air force, and any reserve or auxiliary force of any of those services which has been called out on permanent service, or called into actual service, or embodied;
"assigned matter" means any matter in relation to which the Commissioners are for the time being required in pursuance of any enactment to perform any duties;
"boarding station" means a boarding station for the time being appointed under section 19 below;
"boundary" means the land boundary of Northern Ireland;

"British ship" means a British ship within the meaning of the Merchant Shipping Act 1995. so, however, as not to include a ship registered in any country other than the United Kingdom, the Channel Islands, the Isle of Man or a colony within the meaning of the British Nationality Act 1948;

"claimant", in relation to proceedings for the condemnation of any thing as being forfeited, means a person claiming that the thing is not liable to forfeiture;

"coasting ship" has the meaning given by section 69 below;

"commander", in relation to an aircraft, includes any person having or taking the charge or command of the aircraft;

"the Commissioners" means the Commissioners of Customs and Excise;

"Community transit goods" —

    (a)   in relation to imported goods, means—

        (i)   goods which have been imported under the internal or external Community transit procedure for transit through the United Kingdom with a view to exportation where the importation was and the transit and exportation are to be part of one Community transit operation; or

        (ii)   goods which have, at the port or airport at which they were imported, been placed under the internal or external Community transit procedure for transit through the United Kingdom with a view to exportation where the transit and exportation are to be part of one Community transit operation;

    (b)   in relation to goods for exportation, means—

        (i)   goods which have been imported as mentioned in paragraph (a)(i) of this definition and are to be exported as part of the Community transit operation in the course of which they were imported; or

        (ii)   goods which have, under the internal or external Community transit procedure, transited the United Kingdom from the port or airport at which they were imported and are to be exported as part of the Community transit operation which commenced at that port or airport and for the purposes of paragraph (a)(i) above the Isle of Man shall be treated as if it were part of the United Kingdom;

"container" includes any bundle or package and any box, cask or other receptacle whatsoever;

"the customs and excise Acts" means the Customs and Excise Acts 1979 and any other enactment for the time being in force relating to customs or excise;

"the Customs and Excise Acts 1979" means—

        this Act,

        the Customs and Excise Duties (General Reliefs) Act 1979,

        the Alcoholic Liquor Duties Act 1979,

        the Hydrocarbon Oil Duties Act 1979,

        the Matches and Mechanical Lighters Duties Act 1979, and

        the Tobacco Products Duty Act 1979;

"customs warehouse" ...

"customs and excise airport" has the meaning given by section 21(7) below;

"customs and excise station" has the meaning given by section 26 below;

"designation order" has the meaning given by section 100A (5);

"drawback goods" means goods in the case of which a claim for drawback has been or is to be made;

"dutiable goods", except in the expression "dutiable or restricted goods", means goods of a class or description subject to any duty of customs or excise, whether or not those goods are in fact chargeable with that duty, and whether or not that duty has been paid thereon;

"dutiable or restricted goods" has the meaning given by section 52 below;

"examination station" has the meaning given by section 22A below;

"excise duty part" has the meaning given by section 1 of the Finance (No. 2) Act 1992.

"excise licence trade" means, subject to subsection (5) below, a trade or business for the carrying on of which an excise licence is required;

"excise warehouse" means a place of security approved by the Commissioners under subsection (1) (whether or not it is also approved under subsection (2)) of section 92 below, and, except in that section, also includes a distiller's warehouse;

"exporter", in relation to goods for exportation or for use as stores, includes the shipper of the goods and any person performing in relation to an aircraft functions corresponding with those of a shipper;

"free zone" has the meaning given by section 100A(2);

"free zone goods" are goods which are within a free zone;

"goods" includes stores and baggage;

"holiday", in relation to any part of the United Kingdom, means any day that is a bank holiday in that part of the United Kingdom under the Banking and Financial Dealings Act 1971, Christmas Day, Good Friday and the day appointed for the purposes of customs and excise for the celebration of Her Majesty's birthday;

"hovercraft" means a hovercraft within the meaning of the Hovercraft Act 1968;

"importer", in relation to any goods at any time between their importation and the time when they are delivered out of charge, includes any owner or other person for the time being possessed of or beneficially interested in the goods and, in relation to goods imported by means of a pipe-line, includes the owner of the pipe-line;

"justice" and "justice of the peace" in Scotland includes a sheriff and in Northern Ireland, in relation to any powers and duties which can under any enactment for the time being in force be exercised and performed only by a resident magistrate, means a resident magistrate;

"land" and "landing", in relation to aircraft, include alighting on water;

"law officer of the Crown" means the Attorney General or for the purpose of criminal proceedings in Scotland, the Lord Advocate or, for the purpose of Civil Proceedings in Scotland, the appropriate Law Officer within the meaning of section 4A of the Crown Suits (Scotland) Act 1857 or in Northern Ireland the Attorney General for Northern Ireland;

"licence year", in relation to an excise licence issuable annually, means the period of 12 months ending on the date on which that licence expires in any year;

"master", in relation to a ship, includes any person having or taking the charge or command of the ship;

"nautical mile" ...

"night" means the period between 11 pm and 5 am;

"occupier", in relation to any bonded premises, includes any person who has given security to the Crown in respect of those premises;

"officer" means, subject to section 8(2) below, a person commissioned by the Commissioners;

"owner", in relation to an aircraft, includes the operator of the aircraft;

"owner", in relation to a pipe-line, means (except in the case of a pipe-line vested in the Crown which in pursuance of arrangements in that behalf is operated by another) the person in whom the line is vested and, in the said excepted case, means the person operating the line;

"perfect entry" ...

"pipe-line" has the meaning given by section 65 of the Pipe-lines Act 1962 (that Act being taken, for the purposes of this definition, to extend to Northern Ireland);

"port" means a port appointed by the Commissioners under section 19 below;

"prescribed area" means such an area in Northern Ireland adjoining the boundary as the Commissioners may by regulations prescribe;

"prescribed sum", in relation to the penalty provided for an offence, has the meaning given by section 171(2) below;

"prohibited or restricted goods" means goods of a class or description of which the importation, exportation or carriage coastwise is for the time being prohibited or restricted under or by virtue of any enactment;

"proper", in relation to the person by, with or to whom, or the place at which, anything is to be done, means the person or place appointed or authorised in that behalf by the Commissioners;

"proprietor", in relation to any goods, includes any owner, importer, exporter, shipping or other person for the time being possessed of or beneficially interested in those goods;

"Queen's warehouse" means any place provided by the Crown or appointed by the Commissioners for the deposit of goods for security thereof and of the duties chargeable thereon;

"registered excise dealer and shipper" means a revenue trader approved and registered by the commissioners under section 100a below;

"registered excise dealers and shippers regulations" means regulations under section 100a below;

"representative", in relation to any person from whom the Commissioners assess an amount as being excise duty due, means his personal representative, trustee in bankruptcy or interim or permanent trustee, any receiver or liquidator appointed in relation to him or any of his property or any other person acting in a representative capacity in relation to him;

"the revenue trade provisions of the customs and excise Acts" means—

    (a)   the provisions of the customs and excise Acts relating to the protection, security, collection or management of the revenues derived from the duties of excise on goods produced or manufactured in the United Kingdom;

    (b)   the provisions of the customs and excise Acts relating to any activity or facility for the carrying on or provision of which an excise licence is required;

    (c)   the provisions of the Betting and Gaming Duties Act 1981 (so far as not included in paragraph (b) above);

    (d)   the provisions of Chapter II of Part I of the Finance Act 1993;

    (e)   the provisions of sections 10 to 15 of and Schedule 1 to the Finance Act 1997

"revenue trader" means

    (a)   any person carrying on a trade or business subject to any of the revenue trade provisions of the customs and excise Acts or which consists of or includes—.

        (i)   the buying, selling, importation, exportation, dealing in or handling of any goods of a class or description which is subject to a duty of excise (whether or not duty is chargeable on the goods),

(ia) the buying, selling, importation, exportation, dealing in or handling of tickets or chances on the taking of which lottery duty is or will be chargeable.

(ib) being (without the meaning of sections 10 to 15 of the Finance Act 1997) the provided of any premises for gaming;

(ic) the organisation management or promotion of any gaming (within the meaning of the Gaming Act 1968 or the Betting, Gaming, Lotteries and Amusements (Northern Ireland) Order 1985) or

(ii) the financing or facilitation of any such transactions or activities as are mentioned in sub-paragraph (i), (ia), (ib) or (ic). whether or not that trade or business is an excise licence trade,

(b) any person who is a wholesaler or an occupier of an excise warehouse (so far as not included in paragraph (a) above), and includes a registered club.

"ship" and "vessel" include any boat or other vessel whatsoever (and, to the extent provided in section 2 below, any hovercraft);

"shipment" includes loading into an aircraft, and "shipped" and cognate expressions shall be construed accordingly;

"stores" means, subject to subsection (4) below, goods for use in a ship or aircraft and includes fuel and spare parts and other articles of equipment, whether or not for immediate fitting;

"tons register" means the tons of a ship's net tonnage as ascertained and registered according to the tonnage regulations of the Merchant Shipping Act 1995 or, in the case of a ship which is not registered under that Act, ascertained in like manner as if it were to be so registered;

"transit goods", except in the expression "Community transit goods", means imported goods entered on importation for transit or transhipment;

"transit or transhipment", in relation to the entry of goods, means transit through the United Kingdom or transhipment with a view to the re-exportation of the goods in question or transhipment of those goods for use as stores;

"transit shed" has the meaning given by section 25A below;

"United Kingdom Waters" means any waters (including inland waters) within the seaward limits of the territorial sea of the United Kingdom.

"vehicle" includes a railway vehicle;

"virtualling warehouse" means a place of security approved by the Commissioners under subsection (2) (whether or not it is also a place approved under subsection (1) of section 92 below).

"warehouse", except in the expressions "Queen's warehouse" and

"distiller's warehouse", means a place of security approved by the Commissioners under subsection (1) or (2) or subsections (1) and (2) of section 92 below and, except in that section, also includes a distiller's warehouse; and "warehoused" and cognate expressions shall, subject to subsection (4) of that section and any regulations made by virtue of section 93(2)(da)(i) or (ee) or (4) below be construed accordingly;

"warehousing regulations" means regulations under section 93 below.

(2) This Act and the other Acts included in the Customs and Excise Acts 1979 shall be construed as one Act but where a provision of this Act refers to

this Act that reference is not to be construed as including a reference to any of the others.

(3) Any expression used in this Act or in any instrument made under this Act to which a meaning is given by any other Act included in the Customs and Excise Acts 1979 has, except where the context otherwise requires, the same meaning in this Act or any such instrument as in that Act; and for ease of reference the Table below indicates the expressions used in this Act to which a meaning is given by any other such Act—

Alcoholic Liquor Duties Act 1979

"beer"
"brewer" and "brewer for sale"
"cider"
"compounder"
"distiller"
"distiller's warehouse"
"dutiable alcoholic liquor"
"licensed", in relation to producers of wine or made-wine
"made-wine"
"producer of made-wine"
"producer of wine"
"proof"
"rectifier"
"registered club"
"spirits"
"wholesaler"
"wine"

Hydrocarbon Oil Duties Act 1979

"rebate"
"refinery"

Tobacco Products Duty Act 1979

"tobacco products"

(4) Goods for use in a ship or aircraft as merchandise for sale to persons carried in the ship or aircraft shall be treated for the purposes of the customs and excise Acts as stores if, and only if—

(a) the goods are to be sold by retail either
    (i) in the course of a relevant journey, or
    (ii) for consumption on board; and
(b) the goods are not treated as exported by virtue of regulations under section 12 of the Customs and Excise Duties (General Reliefs) Act 1979 (goods for use in naval ships or establishments).

(4A) For the purposes of subsection (4) above a relevant journey is any journey beginning in the United Kingdom and having an immediate destination outside the member States.

(4B) In relation to goods treated as stores by virtue of subsection (4) above, any reference in the customs and excise Acts to the consumption of stores shall be construed as referring to the sale of the goods as mentioned in paragraph (a) of that subsection.

(5) A person who deals in or sells tobacco products in the course of a trade or business carried on by him shall be deemed for the purposes of this Act to be carrying on an excise licence trade (and to be a revenue trader) notwithstanding that no excise licence is required for carrying on that trade or business.

(6) In computing for the purposes of this Act any period expressed therein

as a period of clear days no account shall be taken of the day of the event from which the period is computed or of any Sunday or holiday.

(7) The provisions of this Act in so far as they relate to customs duties apply, notwithstanding that any duties are imposed for the benefit of the Communities, as if the revenue from duties so imposed remained part of the revenues of the Crown.

AMENDMENTS

Section 1 as amended by the Isle of Man Act 1979 (c.58), Sch.1 para.2, the Finance Act 1981 (c.35), Sch.8 para.1 and Sch.19 Pt 1, the Betting and Gaming Duties Act 1981 (c.63), Sch.5 para 5(a), the Finance Act 1984 (c.43), Sch.4, Pt 2, para.1, the Terroritorial Sea Act 1987 (c.49), Sch.1, para.4(1) and Sch.2, the Finance (No.2) Act 1987 (c.51) s.103(3), the Finance Act 1991 (c.31) s.11(1), (2), the Customs Controls on Importation of Goods Regulations 1991 (SI 1991/ 2724) reg.6(2)(a), 6(2)(b) and 6(2)(c), the Customs Warehousing Regulations 1991 (SI 1991 No. 2725) reg. 3(2)(a)and (b), the Finance (No. 2) Act 1992 (c.48), Sch.1, para.1, Sch.2 para.1(a) and (b), the Customs and Excise (Single Market, etc.) Regulations 1992 (SI 1992/3095) reg.3(1), the Finance Act 1993 (c.34), s.30(2)(a), (b), s.30(3)(b), (c) and Sch.23, Pt 1, para.7, the Value Added Tax Act 1994 (c.23), Sch.14, para.6, the Merchant Shipping Act 1995 (c.21), Sch.13, para.53(2)(a) and (b), the Finance Act 1997 (c.16), Sch.2, para.2(2), (3), (4), Sch.6, para.2(4) and Sch.18, Pt 2 (effective from March 19, 1997), the Scotland Act 1998 (Consequential Modifications) (No. 1) Order 1999 (SI 1999/1042) art.4, Sch.2, para.6 (effective from May 20, 1999), the Finance Act 1999, (c.16), s.10 (effective from July 1, 1999).

. . .

Time of importation, exportation, etc.

5. —(1) The provisions of this section shall have effect for the purposes of the customs and excise Acts.

(2) Subject to subsections (3) and (6) below, the time of importation of any goods shall be deemed to be—

    (a) where the goods are brought by sea, the time when the ship carrying them comes within the limits of a port:

    (b) where the goods are brought by air, the time when the aircraft carrying them lands in the United Kingdom or the time when the goods are unloaded in the United Kingdom, whichever is the earlier;

    (c) where the goods are brought by land, the time when the goods are brought across the boundary into Northern Ireland.

(3) In the case of goods brought by sea of which entry is not required under Regulation 5 of the Customs Controls on Importation of Goods Regulations 1991, the time of importation shall be deemed to be the time when the ship carrying them came within the limits of the port at which the goods are discharged.

(4) Subject to subsections (5) and (7) below, the time of exportation of any goods from the United Kingdom shall be deemed to be—

    (a) where the goods are exported by sea or air, the time when the goods are shipped for exportation;

    (b) where the goods are exported by land, the time when they are cleared by the proper officer at the last customs and excise station on their way to the boundary.

(5) In the case of goods of a class or description with respect to the exportation of which any prohibition or restriction is for the time being in force under or by virtue of any enactment which are exported by sea or air, the time of exportation shall be deemed to be the time when the exporting ship or aircraft departs from the last port or customs and excise airport at which it is cleared before departing for a destination outside the United Kingdom.

(6) Goods imported by means of a pipe-line shall be treated as imported at the time when they are brought within the limits of a port or brought across the boundary into Northern Ireland.

(7) Goods exported by means of a pipe-line shall be treated as exported at the time when they are charged into that pipe-line for exportation.

(8) A ship shall be deemed to have arrived at or departed from a port at the time when the ship comes within or, as the case may be, leaves the limits of that port.

AMENDMENT

Subs.(3) as amended by the Customs and Excise (Single Market etc.) Regulations 1992 (SI 1992/3095) reg.10(1) and Sch.1, para.3.

GENERAL NOTE

In *MacNeil v H.M. Advocate*, 1986 S.C.C.R. 288 the High Court held that in a prosecution under s.50 of the 1979 Act, there was no good reason to regard the act of importation as being capable of occurring within the first United Kingdom appointed port entered by the vessel. Importation occurred at the port where the goods were discovered and at any port in the United Kingdom entered en route to that port.

. . .

Penalty for improper importation of goods

50. — (1) Subsection (2) below applies to goods of the following descriptions, that is to say—
(a) goods chargeable with a duty which has not been paid; and
(b) goods the importation, landing or unloading of which is for the time being prohibited or restricted by or under any enactment.

(2) If any person with intent to defraud Her Majesty of any such duty or to evade any such prohibition or restriction as is mentioned in subsection (1) above—
(a) unships or lands in any port or unloads from any aircraft in the United Kingdom or from any vehicle in Northern Ireland any goods to which this subsection applies, or assists or is otherwise concerned in such unshipping, landing or unloading; or
(b) removes from their place of importation or from any approved wharf, examination station, transit shed or customs and excise station any goods to which this subsection applies or assists or is otherwise concerned in such removal,
he shall be guilty of an offence under this subsection and may be detained.

(3) If any person imports or is concerned in importing any goods contrary to any prohibition or restriction for the time being in force under or by virtue of any enactment with respect to those goods, whether or not the goods are unloaded, and does so with intent to evade the prohibition or restriction, he shall be guilty of an offence under this subsection and may be detained.

(4) Subject to subsection (5) (5A) or (5B) below, a person guilty of an offence under subsection (2) or (3) above shall be liable—
(a) on summary conviction, to a penalty of the prescribed sum or of three times the value of the goods, whichever is the greater, or to imprisonment for a term not exceeding 6 months, or to both; or
(b) on conviction on indictment, to a penalty of any amount, or to imprisonment for a term not exceeding 7 years or to both.

(5) In the case of an offence under subsection (2) or (3) above in connection with a prohibition or restriction on importation having effect by virtue of section 3 of the Misuse of Drugs Act 1971, subsection (4) above shall have effect subject to the modifications specified in Schedule 1 to this Act.

(5A)   In the case of an offence under subsection (2) or (3) above in connection with the prohibition contained in section 20 of the Forgery and Counterfeiting Act 1981, subsection (4)(b) above shall have effect as if for the words "2 years" there were substituted the words "10 years".

(5B)   In the case of an offence under subsection (2) or (3) above in connection with the prohibition contained in regulation 2 of the Import of Seal Skins Regulation 1996, subsection (4) above shall have effect as if—

(a)   for paragraph (a) there were substituted the following—(a) an summary conviction, to a fine not exceeding the statutory maximum or to imprisonment for a term not exceeding three months or to both and

(b)   in paragraph (b) for the words "7 years" there were substituted the words "2 years".

(6)   If any person—

(a)   imports or causes to be imported any goods concealed in a container holding goods of a different description; or

(b)   directly or indirectly imports or causes to be imported or entered any goods found, whether before or after delivery, not to correspond with the entry made thereof,he shall be liable on summary conviction to a penalty of three times the value of the goods or £100, whichever is the greater.

(7)   In any case where a person would, apart from this subsection, be guilty of—

(a)   an offence under this section in connection with the importation of goods contrary to a prohibition or restriction; and

(b)   a corresponding offence under the enactment or other instrument imposing the prohibition or restriction, being an offence for which a fine or other penalty is expressly provided by that enactment or other instrument,he shall not be guilty of the offence mentioned in paragraph (a) of this subsection.

he shall not be guilty of the offence mentioned in paragraph (a) of this subsection.

AMENDMENTS

Subs.(5A) inserted by the Forgery and Counterfeiting Act 1981 (c.45) s.23(1).
Subs.(4)(b) as amended by the Finance Act 1988 (c.39) s.12(1).
Subs.(5B) inserted, and subs.(4) amended, by the Import of Seal Skins Regulations 1996 (SI 1996/2686) reg.4(1).

GENERAL NOTE

Subss.(2) and (3), as subs.(1) makes plain, strike at two different problems. The first is defrauding the Crown of duty on goods which are lawfully within the United Kingdom. Unshipping or landing, or assisting in such conduct or otherwise being concerned in such conduct, of dutiable goods with intent to defraud the Crown of the duty due on them, or removing, assisting in or otherwise being concerned in the removal of such goods from their place of importation are offences triable on both summary complaint and indictment (subs.(4)). The second mischief is dealt with in subs.(3), namely importing or being concerned in importing goods subject to a prohibition or restriction on their importation with intent to evade that prohibition or restriction. Such offence is prosecutable either summarily or on indictment.

Both types of offence require *mens rea* so that the Crown will bear the onus of establishing that the accused intended by the commission of the various acts to defraud the Crown of the duty or to evade the prohibition or restriction on importation. The accused need not be proved to have known the specific identity of the goods but merely to have been aware that they, whatever they were, were liable to duty or the subject of a prohibition or restriction (see *R v Forbes (Giles)* [2001] 3 W.L.R. 428).

It is apparently not the practice in Scotland for the Crown to indict importation offences involving controlled drugs under this provision. In England the prosecution of such offences is often undertaken by H.M. Commissioners of Customs and Excise and it has been observed that they also prefer indictments charging importation under s.170 because offences under that section "are so all-embracing that it is difficult to see when it would be necessary, or tactically advantageous, to rely on s.50" (Archbold, *Criminal Pleading, Evidence and Practice* (2002 ed.), para.25–389).

Subs.(6), however, contains no words importing a mental element in the commission of the offence (unless "concealed" in para.(b) can be given an intentional construction). The offence is clearly of a regulatory nature, as the restriction of the penalty to a fine indicates. Its use might be questionable. Where the offence is discovered and the goods are neither dutiable nor subject to a prohibition or restriction, prosecution can perhaps appear pointless except to give warning *pour encourager les autres*: everything brought into the United Kingdom should be recognisable for what it is so that the Customs authorities can regulate matters and that purpose requires persons entering the country to take care to avoid misdescription. English law now recognises, as it had previously failed on occasion to do, that there is a strong general presumption in favour of *mens rea* being required for statutory offences (see *B (A Minor) v DPP* [2000] 2 A.C. 428). The offence in para.(a) might therefore be capable of construction as importing a mental element by the use of the word "concealed" thereby requiring proof of an intention to import concealed goods (*e.g.* controlled drugs inside a container of prescription drugs) but para.(b) seems only to be capable of importing *mens rea* if one disregards both the regulatory nature of the offence and the modest non-custodial penalty as well as the absence of words of knowledge or intent. The Scottish courts traditionally take a different approach to such an issue and might simply allow a defence of innocent misdescription if the accused raises it in evidence and the court is thereby caused to entertain a reasonable doubt.

Subs.(5) makes specific provision for different penalties to be available in respect of the importation of controlled drugs. Schedule 1 differentiates between Class A and Class B drugs on the one hand and Class C drugs on the other hand. The sentencing judge will be entitled, however, to take into account acceptable evidence that the accused mistakenly believed that he was importing a Class C drug when determining the appropriate sentence (see *Howarth v H.M. Advocate*, 1992 S.C.C.R. 525 at 528D; see also *R. v Bilinski* (1988) 9 Cr. App. R. (S.) 360).

...

Offences in relation to exportation of prohibited or restricted goods

68. —(1) If any goods are—

(a) exported or shipped as stores; or

(b) brought to any place in the United Kingdom for the purpose of being exported or shipped as stores, and the exportation or shipment is or would be contrary to any prohibition or restriction for the time being in force with respect to those goods under or by virtue of any enactment, the goods shall be liable to forfeiture and the exporter or intending exporter of the goods and any agent of his concerned in the exportation or shipment or intended exportation or shipment shall each be liable on summary conviction to a penalty of three times the value of the goods or £100, whichever is the greater.

(2) Any person knowingly concerned in the exportation or shipment as stores, or in the attempted exportation or shipment as stores, of any goods with intent to evade any such prohibition or restriction as is mentioned in subsection (1) above shall be guilty of an offence under this subsection and may be detained.

(3) Subject to subsection (4)–(4A) below, a person guilty of an offence under subsection (2) above shall be liable—

(a) on summary conviction, to a penalty of the prescribed sum or of three times the value of the goods, whichever is the greater, or to imprisonment for a term not exceeding 6 months, or to both; or

(b) on conviction on indictment, to a penalty of any amount, or to imprisonment for a term not exceeding 7 years or to both.

(4) In the case of an offence under subsection (2) above in connection with a prohibition or restriction on exportation having effect by virtue of section 3 of the Misuse of Drugs Act 1971, subsection (3) above shall have effect subject to the modifications specified in Schedule 1 to this Act.

(4A) In the case of an offence under subsection (2) above in connection with the prohibition contained in section 21 of the Forgery and Counterfeiting Act 1981, subsection 3(b) above shall have effect as it for the words "2 years" there were substituted the words "10 years".

(5) If by virtue of any such restriction as is mentioned in subsection (1) above any goods may be exported only when consigned to a particular place or person and any goods so consigned are delivered to some other place or person, the ship, aircraft or vehicle in which they were exported shall be liable to forfeiture unless it is proved to the satisfaction of the Commissioners that both the owner of the ship, aircraft or vehicle and the master of the ship, commander of the aircraft or person in charge of the vehicle—

(a) took all reasonable steps to secure that the goods were delivered to the particular place to which or person to whom they were consigned; and

(b) did not connive at or, except under duress, consent to the delivery of the goods to that other place or person.

(6) In any case where a person would, apart from this subsection, be guilty of—

(a) an offence under subsection (1) or (2) above; and

(b) a corresponding offence under the enactment or instrument imposing the prohibition or restriction in question, being an offence for which a fine or other penalty is expressly provided by that enactment or other instrument,he shall not be guilty of the offence mentioned in paragraph (a) of this subsection.

Amendments

Subs.(3) as amended by the Forgery and Counterfeiting Act 1981 (c.45) s.23(2)(a)
Subs.(4A) inserted by s.23(2)(b) of the above Act.
Subs.(3)(b) as amended by the Finance Act 1988 (c.39) s.12(1).

General Note

Subsection (1) creates the offence of exporting or shipping as stores (or in a limited sense, preparing to export or ship as stores) any goods subject to a prohibition or restriction on export and provides two categories of offender and two consequences of such conduct. The two categories of offenders are (1) the exporter or person preparing to export or ship the goods and (2) such person's agent "concerned in the exportation or shipment or intended exportation or shipment". A question arises as to whether the offence is one of strict (or absolute) liability. There are no words clearly importing *mens rea* and (as with the offence in s.50(6)) the offence appears to be regulatory, as the restriction of the penalty to a fine suggests. It seems likely that since the exporter or his agent should know what is and what is not prohibited or restricted, the offence assumes that they will be acting knowingly. Moreover, consideration of the offence provided for in subs.(2) appears to indicate quite clearly that subs.(1) creates a strict liability offence.

Two consequences follow from the conduct. First, both exporter and agent are liable to prosecution on summary complaint and may be fined. Secondly, the goods shall be liable to forfeiture. Forfeiture proceeds under s.139 of, and Sch.3 to, the 1979 Act. The Divisional Court in England has held that forfeiture proceedings are civil in character and therefore do not attract the additional protections of art.6(2) and (3) of the European Convention on Human Rights (see *Goldsmith v Commissioners of Customs and Excise* [2001] T.L.R. 378). However, forfeiture must strike a fair balance between the rights of the individual and the public interest and it must therefore be a proportionate penalty (see *Lindsay v Commissioners of Customs and Excise* [2002] T.L.R. 88).

Subsection (2) requires the Crown to prove (1) that the accused was knowingly concerned in the exportation, shipment or attempted exportation or shipment, of goods which are subject to the prohibition or restriction and (2) that that was done with intent to evade the prohibition or restriction. The double reference to *mens rea* seems unnecessary from the point of view of Scots law since an agent as is mentioned in subs.(1) who knows what he is concerned in cannot surely be ignorant of his principal's intention to evade the prohibition or restriction. However it is conceivable that English law would view it as necessary for the agent to be proved separately to have shared in the intention to evade, especially where there is only an attempt at export or shipment.

Forfeiture is also authorised under subs.(5). Where a destination—whether place or person—other than that which is required to be the destination of consigned goods is found to have been the place of delivery, or the recipient, of the goods then the transport used for export of the goods shall be liable to forfeiture unless the owner proves to the Commissioners' satisfaction that all reasonable steps were taken to deliver to the designated place or person and absence of connivance at or consent to delivery to a different destination or recipient. (The qualification that the consent will be immaterial if shown to have been given under duress would mean in Scots law coerced consent, which would be no consent in law anyway. In such cases the relevant person would require to satisfy the Commissioners that his consent had been forced according to the ordinary requirements of coercion including the use of a threat of serious injury or death.)

This forfeiture provision raises two issues. First, is the imposition of a burden on the owner of the transport to establish both of these facts compatible with art.6 of the European Convention? Secondly, if it is, is the automatic forfeiture following a failure to prove these factors (presumably on balance of probabilities), not likely sometimes to be inconsistent with Art. 1 of the First Protocol to the European Convention? Since the factors appear to go to the excusability of the export to the wrong place or person and thus negate the culpability of the export, it would be possible to argue that the owner was obliged to prove his innocence, if the issue were characterisable as a criminal charge. However, for the reasons given in *Goldsmith v Commissioners of Customs and Excise, supra*, it might be that the Scottish courts would hold that a criminal charge was not in issue. The reverse burden would therefore be arguably acceptable. However, in *International Transport Roth GmbH v Secretary of State for the Home Department* [2001] T.L.R. 673, Sullivan J. held that the focus of the liability to fixed penalties which were imposed on haulage companies and lorry drivers as persons responsible for the clandestine entry of illegal immigrants into the United Kingdom was on the hauliers and drivers' moral culpability and thus made the issue a criminal charge in effect. The Court of Appeal ([2002] T.L.R. 86) did not expressly reverse that assessment but held that the fixed penalties were disproportionate in amount to what was needed in order to achieve improved immigration control. The Court's decision was, however, in essence that "the hallowed principle that the punishment must fit the crime was irreconcilable with the notion of a substantial fixed penalty" and thus the penalty was incompatible with Art. 6, since there could be no room for mitigation.

This reasoning seems applicable to a forfeiture which follows automatically where the transport is of substantial value (as will likely be the case) and the owner fails to establish both factors. For similar reasons it seems likely that Art. 1 of the First Protocol would also be violated since deprivation of the owner's property in the transport would require to be on the basis that it was "necessary to control the use of property in the general interest" and there would therefore require to be a reasonable relationship in terms of proportionality between the means employed and the aim pursued (see *Lindsay v Commissioners of Customs and Excise, supra*). Automatic forfeiture would be likely to be disproportionate in that sense.

...

Penalty for fraudulent evasion of duty, etc.

170. —(1) Without prejudice to any other provision of the Customs and Excise Acts 1979, if any person—
  (a) knowingly acquires possession of any of the following goods, that is to say—
    (i) goods which have been unlawfully removed from a warehouse or Queen's warehouse;
    (ii) goods which are chargeable with a duty which has not been paid;
    (iii) goods with respect to the importation or exportation of which any prohibition or restriction is for the time being in force under or by virtue of any enactment; or
  (b) is in any way knowingly concerned in carrying, removing, depositing, harbouring, keeping or concealing or in any manner dealing with any such goods,and does so with intent to defraud Her Majesty of any duty payable on the goods or to evade any such prohibition or restriction with respect to the goods he shall be guilty of an offence under this section and may be detained.

(2) Without prejudice to any other provision of the Customs and Excise Acts 1979, if any person is, in relation to any goods, in any way knowingly concerned in any fraudulent evasion or attempt at evasion—

(a) of any duty chargeable on the goods;

(b) of any prohibition or restriction for the time being in force with respect to the goods under or by virtue of any enactment; or

(c) of any provision of the Customs and Excise Acts 1979 applicable to the goods,he shall be guilty of an offence under this section and may be detained.

(3) Subject to subsection (4), (4A) or (4B), below, a person guilty of an offence under this section shall be liable—

(a) on summary conviction, to a penalty of the prescribed sum or of three times the value of the goods, whichever is the greater, or to imprisonment for a term not exceeding 6 months, or to both; or

(b) on conviction on indictment, to a penalty of any amount, or to imprisonment for a term not exceeding 7 years, or to both.

(4) In the case of an offence under this section in connection with prohibition or restriction on importation or exportation having effect by virtue of section 3 of the Misuse of Drugs Act 1971, subsection (3) above shall have effect subject to the modifications specified in Schedule 1 to this Act.

(4A) In the case of an offence under this section in connection with the prohibitions contained in sections 20 and 21 of the Forgery and Counterfeiting Act 1981, subsection (3)(b) above shall have effect as if for the words "2 years" there were substituted the words "10 years."

(4B) In the case of an offence under subsection (1) or (2) above in connection with the prohibition contained in regulation 2 of the Import of Seal Skins Regulations 1996, subsection (3) above shall have effect as if—

(a) for paragraph (a) there were substituted the following (a) on summary conviction, to a fine not exceeding the statutory maximum or to imprisonment for a term not exceeding three months, or to both; and

(b) in paragraph (b) for the words "7 years" there were substituted the words "2 years".

(5) In any case where a person would, apart from this subsection, be guilty of—

(a) an offence under this section in connection with a prohibition or restriction; and

(b) a corresponding offence under the enactment or other instrument imposing the prohibition or restriction, being an offence for which a fine or other penalty is expressly provided by that enactment or other instrument,he shall not be guilty of the offence mentioned in paragraph (a) of this subsection.

(6) Where any person is guilty of an offence under this section, the goods in respect of which the offence was committed shall be liable to forfeiture

AMENDMENTS

Subs.(4A) inserted by the Forgery and Counterfeiting Act 1981 (c.45), s.23
Subs.(6) inserted by the Finance (No.2) Act 1992 (c.48), Sch.2, para.7.
Subs.(3) as amended by the Import of Seal Skins Regulations 1996 (SI 1996/2686) reg.4(2)(a).
Subs.(4B) inserted by reg.4(2)(b) of the above Regulations.
Subs.(3)(b) as amended by the Finance Act 1988 (c.39), s.12(1)(a)(b).

GENERAL NOTE

The most commonly encountered offence is that contained in s.170(2)(b), namely being knowingly concerned in any fraudulent evasion or attempt at evasion of any prohibition, in respect of controlled drugs the importation of which is unlawful by virtue of s.3 of the Misuse of Drugs

Act 1971 (c.38). The Crown requires to prove that the accused knew that he was involved in importing something which was prohibited but need not be shown to have been aware that it was a controlled drug (far less a particular controlled drug) (see *Howarth v H.M. Advocate (No.1)*, 1992 S.C.C.R. 364 at 367D). As Lawton, L.J. said: "It matters not for the purpose of conviction what the goods were as long as he knew that he was bringing into the United Kingdom goods which he should not have been bringing in." (*R. v Hennessey* (1978), 68 Cr.App.R. 419 where the offence under consideration was contained in the identically worded s.304(b) of the Customs and Excise Act 1952 (c.44)). Thus where the accused believed that he was importing pornographic goods when in fact the contraband was cannabis (both of which are unlawful), the accused had no defence to conviction (*R. v Ellis* (1987) 84 Cr.App.R. 235). However, if the accused believed that the contraband was currency (the importation of which is not restricted or prohibited), he is entitled to acquittal because he is then not knowingly concerned in a fraudulent evasion (see *R. v Taffe* [1984] A.C. 539). The House of Lords has very recently reaffirmed that the correct approach is that laid down in *Taffe*. In *R. v Forbes (Giles)* [2001] 3 W.L.R. 428 Lord Hope of Craighead stated: "[I]t is not necessary ... for the prosecutor to prove that the defendant knew the identity of the goods which were the subject of the prohibition which he was evading or attempting to evade. It is sufficient for him to prove that [1] that the defendant knew that the goods, whatever they happened to be, were the subject of a prohibition and [2] that he also knew that the operation on which he was engaged was an evasion of that prohibition." (at 433C–D, para.19, numerals added). The essence of the requirement of proof was explained thus: "It is knowledge of the nature and purpose of the *operation* which has to be proved, not knowledge of what the *goods* were which were being brought in to this country." (at 435E, para.26). This approach to the offence was necessary otherwise, as Lord Hutton remarked, the Crown's task would be "virtually impossible" (at 444H, para.57).

The categories of goods which are prohibited and thus capable of being the object of a prosecution under this section are varied. For example, they include goat hair infected or likely to be infected by anthrax (Anthrax Prevention Order 1971) and plants and agricultural products which may lead to the introduction into Great Britain of pests (Plant Health Act 1967, s.2). However European Community law has intruded into this area of domestic regulation. Importation of goods from other member states must be permitted unless their supply would be unlawful under domestic law (*Conegate Ltd v H.M. Customs and Excise* (Case 121/85) [1987] Q.B. 254). The prohibitions remain the the case of goods imported from countries outside the European Union.

The 1979 Act contains no equivalent to s.28(2) and (3) of the Misuse of Drugs Act 1971 (c.38). The use of the word "knowingly" renders the specific provision of statutory defences unnecessary. In the House of Lords *R v Shivpuri* [1987] A.C. 1 it was concluded that the legislature must have assumed from the decision in *R. v Hussain* [1969] 2 Q.B. 567, which was applied by the Court of Appeal in *R v Hennessey* (1978) 68 Cr.App.R. 419, that there was no need for specific defences such as was provided for in the 1971 Act.

The use of the word "fraudulent" has been held by the Court of Appeal in England as not requiring proof of deception practised on Customs officers and others. All that the word requires is dishonest conduct deliberately designed to defeat the prohibition (see *Attorney-General's Reference (No. 1 of 1981)* [1982] Q.B. 848; see also Lord Penrose's charge to the jury in *Howarth v H.M. Advocate (No.1)*, 1992 S.C.C.R. 364 at 367G–368A). There is no need for the accused's criminal state of mind to subsist at the time of importation: it is sufficient that it existed at the time when the accused acted in such a way as to make him knowingly concerned in the evasion of the prohibition (*R v Jakeman* (1983) 76 Cr.App.R. 223). Evasion continues even after the contraband has been seized by the authorities (*R v Green* (1975) 62 Cr.App.R. 74).

Offence of handling goods subject to unpaid excise duty

170A. — (1) Subject to subsection (2) below, if—

(a) after the excise duty point for any goods which are chargeable with a duty of excise, a person acquires possession of those goods or is concerned in carrying, removing, depositing, keeping or otherwise dealing with those goods; and

(b) at the time when he acquires possession of those goods or is so concerned, a payment of duty on the goods is outstanding and has not been deferred,

the conduct of that person falling within paragraph (a) above shall attract a penalty under section 9 of the Finance Act 1994 (civil penalties) which shall be calculated by reference to the amount of the unpaid duty.

(2)   Section 10 of the Finance Act 1994 (exception to civil penalty cases of reasonable excuse) shall not apply in relation to conduct attracting a penalty by virtue of subsection (1) above; but such conduct shall not give rise to any liable to a penalty under section 9 of that Act if the person whose conduct it is satisfies the Commissioners or on appeal, a VAT and duties tribunal, that he—

(a)   acted in accordance with the directions of, or with the consent of, the proper officer: or

(b)   was not himself the person, or one of the persons, liable to pay the unpaid duty and at the time when he acted either—

(i)   had no grounds for suspecting that the goods were chargeable with a duty of excise that had not yet been paid; or

(ii)   believed on reasonable grounds that the duty had been paid or its payment deferred or that the liability to pay the duty had not yet taken effect.

(2A)   In relation to a case involving goods that constitute "shuttle train goods" for the purposes of an order made under sections 11 and 13 of the Channel Tunnel Act 1987, subsections (1) and (2) above shall apply and be construed as if—

(a)   the excise duty point for those goods has been passed, and

(b)   those goods are chargeable with a duty of excise.

AMENDMENTS

Subs.(1)(a) inserted by the Finance (No.2) Act 1992 (c.48), Sch.2 para.8

Subs.(1)(b) as amended by the Finance Act 1994 (c.9), Sch.4, para.13(1)(a).

Subs.(1) as amended by Sch.4, para.13(1)(b) of the above Act.

Subs.(2) substituted by Sch.4, para.13(2) of the above Act.

Subs.(2A) inserted by the Channel Tunnel (Alcoholic Liquor and Tobacco Products) Order 2000 (SI 2000/426), Sch.2, para.2 (effective March 17, 2000).

Offence of taking preparatory steps for evasion of excise duty

170B. —(1) If any person is knowingly concerned in the taking of any steps with a view to the fraudulent evasion, whether by himself or another, of any duty of excise on any goods, he shall be liable—

(a)   on summary conviction, to a penalty of the prescribed sum or of three times the amount of the duty, whichever is the greater, or to imprisonment for a term not exceeding six months or to both; and

(b)   on conviction on indictment, to a penalty of any amount or to imprisonment for a term not exceeding seven years or to both.

(2)   Where any person is guilty of an offence under this section, the goods in respect of which the offence was committed shall be liable to forfeiture."

9.   In section 171(5) of that Act (which provides for the time at which duty is to be treated as payable where that cannot be ascertained for the purposes of any offence)—

(a)   after "43 above" there shall be inserted "or the relevant excise duty point"; and

(b)   at the end there shall be inserted "or, as the case may be, as if the time when the proceedings were commenced was the relevant excise duty point.

AMENDMENTS

Section 170B inserted by the Finance (No.2) Act 1992 (c.48), Sch.2 para.8.

...

SCHEDULES

SCHEDULE 1

CONTROLLED DRUGS: VARIATION OF PUNISHMENTS FOR CERTAIN OFFENCES UNDER THIS ACT

1. Section 50(4), 68(3) and 170(3) of this Act shall have effect in a case where the goods in respect of which the offence referred to in that subsection was committed were a Class A drug or a Class B drug as if for the words from "shall be liable" onwards there were substituted the following words, that is to say—

"shall be liable—
  (a) on summary conviction, to a penalty of the prescribed sum or of three times the value of the goods, whichever is the greater, or to imprisonment for a term not exceeding 6 months, or to both;
  (b) on connection on indictment—
    (i) where the goods were a Class A drug, to a penalty of any amount, or to imprisonment for life, or to both; and
    (ii) where they were a Class B drug, to a penalty of any amount, or to imprisonment for a term not exceeding 14 years, or to both.

2. Section 50(4), 68(3) and 170(3) of this Act shall have effect in a case where the goods in respect of which the offence referred to in that subsection was committed were a Class C drug as if for the words from "shall be liable" onwards there were substituted the following words, that is to say—

"shall be liable—
  (a) on summary conviction in Great Britain, to a penalty of three times the value of the goods or £500, whichever is the greater, or to imprisonment for a term not exceeding 3 months, or to both;
  (b) on summary conviction in Northern Ireland, to a penalty of three times the value of the goods or £100, whichever is the greater, or to imprisonment for a term not exceeding 6 months, or to both;
  (c) on conviction on indictment, to a penalty of any amount, or to imprisonment for a term not exceeding 5 years, or to both.

3. In this Schedule "Class A drug", "Class B drug" and "Class C drug" have the same meanings as in the Misuse of Drugs Act 1971.

AMENDMENTS

Sch.1 as amended by the Controlled Drugs (Penalties) Act 1985 (c.39) s.1(2)
. . .

CRIMINAL JUSTICE (INTERNATIONAL CO-OPERATION) ACT 1990

(1990 c.5)

An Act to enable the United Kingdom to co-operate with other countries in criminal proceedings and investigations; to enable the United Kingdom to join with other countries in implementing the Vienna Convention against Illicit Traffic in Narcotic Drugs and Psychotropic Substances; and to provide for the seizure, detention and forfeiture of drug trafficking money imported or exported in cash.

[5th April 1990]

...

PART II

THE VIENNA CONVENTION

Substances useful for manufacture of controlled drugs

Manufacture and Supply of Schedule Substances

12. — (1) It is an offence for a person—
(a) to manufacture a schedule substance; or
(b) to supply such a substance to another person,

51

knowing or suspecting that the substance is to be used in or for the unlawful production of a controlled drug.

(1A) A person does not commit an offence under subsection (1) above if he manufactures or the case may be, supplies the scheduled substance with the express consent of a constable

(2) A person guilty of an offence under subsection (1) above is liable—

(a) on summary conviction, to imprisonment for a term not exceeding six months or a fine not exceeding the statutory maximum or both;

(b) on conviction on indictment, to imprisonment for a term not exceeding fourteen years or a fine or both.

(3) In this section "a controlled drug" has the same meaning as in the Misuse of Drugs Act, 1971 and "unlawful production of a controlled drug" means the production of such a drug which is unlawful by virtue of section 4(1)(a) of that Act.

(4) In this section and elsewhere in this Part of this Act "a scheduled substance" means a substance for the time being specified in Schedule 2 to this Act.

AMENDMENT

Subs.(1A) inserted by the Criminal Justice (International Co-operation) (Amendment) Act 1998 (c.27) (effective September 9, 1998).

Regulations about scheduled substances

13. —(1) The Secretary of State may by regulations make provision—

(a) imposing requirements as to the documentation of transactions involving scheduled substances;

(b) requiring the keeping of records and the furnishing of information with respect to such substances;

(c) for the inspection of records kept pursuant to the regulations;

(d) for the labelling of consignments of scheduled substances,

(2) Regulations made by virtue of subsection (1)(b) may, in particular, require—

(a) the notification of the proposed exportation of substances specified in Table I in Schedule 2 to this Act to such countries as may be specified in the regulations; and

(b) the production, in such circumstances as may be so specified, of evidence that the required notification has been given;

and for the purposes of section 68 of the Customs and Excise Management Act 1979 (offences relating to exportation of prohibited or restricted goods) any such substance shall be deemed to be exported contrary to a restriction for the time being in force with respect to it under this Act if it is exported without the requisite notification having been given.

(3) Regulations under this section may make different provision in relation to the substances specified in Table I and Table II in Schedule 2 to this Act respectively and in relation to different cases or circumstances.

(4) The power to make regulations under this section shall be exercisable by statutory instrument subject to annulment in pursuance of a resolution of either House of Parliament.

(5) Any person who fails to comply with any requirement imposed by the regulations or, in purported compliance with any such requirement, furnishes information which he knows to be false in a material particular or recklessly furnishes information which is false in a material particular is guilty of an offence and liable—

(a) on summary conviction, to imprisonment for a term not exceeding six months or a fine not exceeding the statutory maximum or both;

(b) on conviction on indictment, to imprisonment for a term not exceeding two years or a fine or both.

(6) No information obtained pursuant to the regulations shall be disclosed except for the purposes of criminal proceedings or of proceedings under the provisions of relating to the confiscation of the proceeds of drug trafficking or corresponding provisions in force in Northern Ireland or of proceedings under Part 2, 3 or 4 of the Proceeds of Crime Act 2002.

AMENDMENT

Subs.(6) as amended by the Proceeds of Crime Act 2002 (c.29), Sch.11, para.21, Sch.12. Brought into force on March 24, 2003 by the Proceeds of Crime Act 2002 (Commencement No.5, Transitional Provisions, Savings and Amendment) Order 2003 (SI 2003/333).

Proceeds of drug trafficking

Concealing or Transferring Proceeds of Drug Trafficking

14. [...]

AMENDMENT

Section 14 repealed by Proceeds of Crime Act 2002 (c.29), Sch.12. Brought into force on February 24, 2003 by the Proceeds of Crime Act 2002 (Commencement No.4, Transitional Provisions and Savings) Order 2003 (SI 2003/120 (C.6)).

Offences at sea

Offences on British Ships

18. Anything which would constitute a drug trafficking offence if done on land in any part of the United Kingdom shall constitute that offence if done on a British ship.

Ships used for Illicit Traffic

19. — (1) This section applies to a British ship, a ship registered in a state other than the United Kingdom which is a party to the Vienna Convention (a "Convention state") and a ship not registered in any country or territory.

(2) A person is guilty of an offence if on a ship to which this section applies, wherever it may be, he—

(a) has a controlled drug in his possession; or

(b) is in any way knowingly concerned in the carrying or concealing of a controlled drug on the ship,

knowing or having reasonable grounds to suspect that the drug is intended to be imported or has been exported contrary to section 3(1) of the Misuse of Drugs Act 1971 or the law of any state other than the United Kingdom.

(3) A certificate purporting to be issued by or on behalf of the government of any state to the effect that the importation or export of a controlled drug is prohibited by the law of that state shall be evidence, and in Scotland sufficient evidence, of the matters stated.

(4) A person guilty of an offence under this section is liable—

(a) in a case where the controlled drug is a Class A drug—

    (i) on summary conviction, to imprisonment for a term not exceeding six months or a fine not exceeding the statutory maximum or both;

    (ii) on conviction on indictment, to imprisonment for life or a fine or both;

(b) in a case where the controlled drug is a Class B drug—

      (i)   on summary conviction, to imprisonment for a term not exceeding six months or a fine not exceeding the statutory maximum or both;

      (ii) on conviction on indictment, to imprisonment for a term not exceeding fourteen years or a fine or both;

  (c) in a case where the controlled drug is a Class C drug—

      (i)   on summary conviction, to imprisonment for a term not exceeding three months or a fine not exceeding the statutory maximum or both;

      (ii) on conviction on indictment, to imprisonment for a term not exceeding five years or a fine or both.

(5) In this section "a controlled drug" and the references to controlled drugs of a specified Class have the same meaning as in the said Act of 1971; and an offence under this section shall be included in the offences to which section 28 of that Act (defences) applies.

Enforcement Powers

20. —(1) The powers conferred on an enforcement officer by Schedule 3 to this Act shall be exercisable in relation to any ship to which section 18 or 19 above applies for the purpose of detecting and the taking of appropriate action in respect of the offences mentioned in those sections.

(2) Those powers shall not be exercised outside the landward limits of the territorial sea of the United Kingdom in relation to a ship registered in a Convention state except with the authority of the Commissioners of Customs and Excise; and they shall not give their authority unless that state has in relation to that state—

  (a) requested the assistance of the United Kingdom for the purpose mentioned in subsection (1) above; or

  (b) authorised the United Kingdom to act for that purpose.

(3) In giving their authority pursuant to a request or authorisation from a Convention state the Commissioners of Customs and Excise shall impose such conditions or limitations on the exercise of the powers as may be necessary to give effect to any conditions or limitations imposed by that state.

(4) The Commissioners of Customs and Excise may, either of their own motion or in response to a request from a Convention state, authorise a Convention state to exercise, in relation to a British ship, powers corresponding to those conferred on enforcement officers by Schedule 3 to this Act but subject to such conditions or limitations, if any, as they may impose.

(5) Subsection (4) above is without prejudice to any agreement made, or which may be made, on behalf of the United Kingdom whereby the United Kingdom undertakes not to object to the exercise by any other state in relation to a British ship of powers corresponding to those conferred by that Schedule.

(6) The powers conferred by that Schedule shall not be exercised in the territorial sea of any state other than the United Kingdom without the authority of the Commissioners of Customs and Excise and they shall not give their authority unless that state has consented to the exercise of those powers.

AMENDMENT

Subss.(2), (3), (4) and (6) as amended by the Criminal Justice Act 1993 (c.36) s.23(2)(a).

Jurisdiction and Prosecutions

21. —(1) Proceedings under this Part of this Act or Schedule 3 in respect of an offence on a ship may be taken, and the offence may for all incidental purposes be treated as having been committed, in any place in the United Kingdom.

(2) ...

(3) Without prejudice to subsection (2) above no proceedings for an offence under Section 19 above alleged to have been committed outside the landward limits of the territorial sea of the United Kingdom on a ship registered in a Convention state shall be instituted except in pursuance of the exercise with the authority of the Commissioners of Customs and Excise of the powers conferred by Schedule 3 to this Act; and Section 3 of the Territorial Waters Jurisdiction Act 1878 (consent of Secretary of State for certain prosecutions) shall not apply to those proceedings.

AMENDMENTS

Subs.(3) as amended by the Criminal Justice Act 1993 (c.36) s.23(2)(b).

...

Extension of certain offences to Crown servants and exemptions for regulators etc.

23A — (1) The Secretary of State may by regulations provide that, in such circumstances as may be prescribed, Section 14(2) above shall apply to such persons in the public service of the Crown, or such categories of person in that service, as may be prescribed.

...

(5) In this section—
"the Crown" includes the Crown in right of Her Majesty's Government in Northern Ireland; and
"prescribed" means prescribed by regulations made by the Secretary of State.

...

AMENDMENT

Section 23A inserted by the Criminal Justice Act 1993 (c.36) Sch.4, para.5.

SCHEDULES

...

Sections 12 and 13   SCHEDULE 2

SUBSTANCES USEFUL FOR MANUFACTURING CONTROLLED DRUGS

TABLE 1

N-Acetylanthranilic acid	3,4-Methylenedioxyphenyl-2-
Ephedrine	propanone
Ergometrine	1-Phenyl-2-propanone
Ergotamine	Piperonal
Isosafrole	Pseudoephedrine
Lysergic acid	Safrole

The salts of the substances listed in this Table whenever the existence of such salts is possible.

TABLE 2

Acetic anhydride	Phenylacetic acid
Acetone	Piperidine
Anthranilic acid	Potassium Permanganate
Ethyl ether	Sulphuric acid
Hydrochloric acid	Toluene
Methyl ethyl ketone	

The salts of the substances listed in this Table except hydrochloric acid and sulphuric acid whenever the existence of such salts is possible.

Section 20   SCHEDULE 3

ENFORCEMENT POWERS IN RESPECT OF SHIPS

Preliminary

1. — (1) In this Schedule "an enforcement officer" means—
   (a)   a constable;
   (b)   an officer commissioned by the Commissioners of Customs and Excise under Section 6(3) of the Customs and Excise Management Act, 1979; and
   (c)   any other person of a description specified in an order made for the purposes of this Schedule by the Secretary of State.

(2) The power to make an order under sub-paragraph (1)(c) above shall be exercisable by statutory instrument subject to annulment in pursuance of a resolution of either House of Parliament.

(3) In this Schedule "the ship" means the ship in relation to which the powers conferred by this Schedule are exercised.

Power to Stop, Board, Divert and Detain

2. — (1) An enforcement officer may stop the ship, board it and, if he thinks it necessary for the exercise of his functions, require it to be taken to a port in the United Kingdom and detain it there.

(2) Where an enforcement officer is exercising his powers with the authority of the Commissioners of Customs and Excise given under section 20(2) of this Act the officer may require the ship to be taken to a port in the Convention state in question or, if that state has so requested, in any other country or territory willing to receive it.

(3) For any of those purpose he may require the master or any member of the crew to take such action as may be necessary.

(4) If an enforcement officer detains a vessel he shall serve on the master a notice in writing stating that it is to be detained until the notice is withdrawn by the service on him of a further notice in writing signed by an enforcement officer.

Power to Search and Obtain information

3. — (1) An enforcement officer may search the ship, anyone on it and anything on it including its cargo.

(2) An enforcement officer may require any person on the ship to give information concerning himself or anything on the ship.

(3) Without prejudice to the generality of those powers an enforcement officer may—
   (a)   open any containers;
   (b)   make tests and take samples of anything on the ship;
   (c)   require the production of documents, books or records relating to the ship or anything on it;
   (d)   make photographs or copies of anything whose production he has power to require.

Powers in Respect of Suspected Offence

4. If an enforcement officer has reasonable grounds to suspect that an offence mentioned in section 18 or 19 of this Act has been committed on a ship to which that section applies he may—
   (a)   arrest without warrant anyone whom he has reasonable grounds for suspecting to be guilty of the offence; and

    (b) seize and detain anything found on the ship which appears to him to be evidence of the offence.

Assistants

5. — (1) An enforcement officer may take with him, to assist him in exercising his powers—
    (a) any other persons; and
    (b) any equipment or materials.

(2) A person whom an enforcement officer takes with him to assist him may perform any of the officer's functions but only under the officer's supervision.

Use of Reasonable Force

6. An enforcement officer may use reasonable force, if necessary, in the performance of his functions.

Evidence of Authority

7. An enforcement officer shall, if required, produce evidence of his authority.

Protection of Officers

8. An enforcement officer shall not be liable in any civil or criminal proceedings for anything done in the purported performance of his functions under this Schedule if the court is satisfied that the act was done in good faith and that there were reasonable grounds for doing it.

Offences

9. — (1) A person is guilty of an offence if he—
    (a) intentionally obstructs an enforcement officer in the performance of any of his functions under this Schedule;
    (b) fails without reasonable excuse to comply with a requirement made by an enforcement officer in the performance of those functions; or
    (c) in purporting to give information required by an officer for the performance of those functions—
        (i) makes a statement which he knows to be false in a material particular or recklessly makes á statement which is false in a material particular; or
        (ii) intentionally fails to disclose any material particular.

(2) A person guilty of an offence under this paragraph is liable on summary conviction to a fine not exceeding level 5 on the standard scale.

CRIMINAL LAW (CONSOLIDATION) (SCOTLAND) ACT 1995

(1995 c.39)

An Act to consolidate for Scotland certain enactments creating offences and relating to criminal law there.

[8th November 1995]

PART II

SPORTING EVENTS: CONTROL OF ALCOHOL ETC.

General Note

[1] This Part of the Act is derived from Pt V of the Criminal Justice (Scotland) Act 1980 (which was enacted as a result of the Report of the McElhone Working Group on Football Crowd Behaviour), and the Sporting Events (Control of Alcohol etc.) Act 1985, both as amended and provides mechanisms for the control of alcohol at sporting events when the event or ground is designated by the Secretary of State.

PARLIAMENTARY DEBATES FOR THE SPORTING EVENTS (CONTROL OF ALCOHOL ETC.) ACT 1985 (c.57)

Hansard, H.C. Vol.81, col.919; Vol.82, col.333; Vol.83, col.758; H.L. Vol.465, col.1313; Vol.466, cols 322 and 751.

Designation of sports grounds and sporting events

18. —(1) Subject to subsection (2) below, the Secretary of State may for the purposes of this Part of this Act by order designate—
 (a) a sports ground or a class of sports ground;
 (b) a sporting event, or a class of sporting event, at that ground or at any of that class of ground;
 (c) a sporting event, or a class of sporting event, taking place outside Great Britain.
 (2) An order under this section shall not apply to a sporting event at which all the participants take part without financial or material reward and to which all spectators are admitted free of charge; but this subsection is without prejudice to the order's validity as respects any other sporting event.
 (3) The power to make an order under subsection (1) above shall be exercisable by statutory instrument which shall be subject to annulment in pursuance of a resolution of either House of Parliament.

DEFINITIONS

 "sports ground": s.23.
 "sporting event": s.23.

---

[1] Annotations by Robert Shiels, Solicitor.

The Sports Grounds and Sporting Events (Designation) (Scotland) Order 1998 (SI 1998/2314 (S.121)) came into force on October 13, 1998. This Order designates the sports grounds, the classes of sporting events played at those grounds and the classes of sporting events outside Great Britain for the purposes of Part II of the Criminal Law (Consolidation) (Scotland) Act 1995. The 1998 Order revoked the earlier 1985 Order and various subsequent Orders following on from 1985.

Alcohol on vehicles

19. — (1) Where a public service vehicle or railway passenger vehicle is being operated for the principal purpose of conveying passengers for the whole or part of a journey to or from a designated sporting event, then—

(a) any person in possession of alcohol on the vehicle shall be guilty of an offence and liable on summary conviction to imprisonment for a period not exceeding 60 days or a fine not exceeding level 3 on the standard scale or both;

(b) if alcohol is being carried on the vehicle and the vehicle is on hire to a person, he shall, subject to subsection (7) below, be guilty of an offence and liable on summary conviction to a fine not exceeding level 3 on the standard scale; and

(c) any person who is drunk on the vehicle shall be guilty of an offence and liable on summary conviction to a fine not exceeding level 2 on the standard scale.

(2) Notwithstanding section 92 of the Licensing (Scotland) Act 1976 (restriction on carriage of alcoholic liquor in crates on contract carriages), but subject to subsection (7) below, if the operator of a public service vehicle which is being operated as mentioned in subsection (1) above, either by himself or by his employee or agent permits alcohol to be carried on the vehicle, the operator and, as the case may be, the employee or agent shall be guilty of an offence and liable on summary conviction to a fine not exceeding level 3 on the standard scale:

(3) This subsection applies to a motor vehicle which is not a public service vehicle but which is adapted to carry more than 8 passengers and is being operated for the principal purpose of conveying two or more passengers for the whole or part of a journey to or from a designated sporting event.

(4) Any person in possession of alcohol on a vehicle to which subsection (3) above applies shall be guilty of an offence and liable on summary conviction to imprisonment for a period not exceeding 60 days or a fine not exceeding level 3 on the standard scale or both.

(5) Any person who is drunk on a vehicle to which subsection (3) above applies shall be guilty of an offence and liable on summary conviction to a fine not exceeding level 2 on the standard scale.

(6) Any person who permits alcohol to be carried on a vehicle to which subsection (3) above applies and—

(a) is the driver of the vehicle; or

(b) where he is not its driver, is the keeper of the vehicle, the employee or agent of the keeper, a person to whom it is made available (by hire, loan or otherwise) by the keeper or the keeper's employee or agent, or the employee or agent of a person to whom it is so made available,

shall, subject to subsection (7) below, be guilty of an offence and liable on summary conviction to a fine not exceeding level 3 on the standard scale.

(7) Where a person is charged with an offence under subsection (1)(b), (2) or (6) above, it shall be a defence for him to prove that the alcohol was car-

ried on the vehicle without his consent or connivance and that he did all he reasonably could to prevent such carriage.

AMENDMENT

Subs.(3) as amended by the Crime and Punishment (Scotland) Act 1997 (c.48), s.62(1) and Sch.1, para.18(4); brought into force by the Crime and Punishment (Scotland) Act 1997 (Commencement and Transitional Provisions) Order 1997 (SI 1997/1712), para.3 (August 1, 1997).

DEFINITIONS

"alcohol": s.23; Licensing (Scotland) Act 1976 (c.66), s.139.
"operation": s.23.
"public service vehicle": s.23.
"railway passenger vehicle": s.23.
"standard scale": Criminal Procedure (Scotland) Act 1995 (c.46), s.225.
"the 1980 Act": Criminal Justice (Scotland) Act 1980 (c.62).

GENERAL NOTE

Subs.(2)

This section makes the operator vicariously liable for the actings of his employee or agent. There is a defence of "due diligence" contained in subs.(7).

Subss.(3)–(5) and (6)

These subsections create similar provisions to subss.(1) and (2), applicable to vehicles falling outwith the definition of "public service vehicle" or "railways passenger vehicle" but adapted to carry more than eight passengers and being operated for the purpose of taking two or more people to a designated event. These provisions were added to the 1980 Act by the Public Order Act 1986.

Sporting events: controls

20. — (1) Any person who—

(a) is in possession of a controlled container in; or

(b) while in possession of a controlled container, attempts to enter, the relevant area of a designated sports ground at any time during the period of a designated sporting event shall be guilty of an offence and liable on summary conviction to imprisonment for a period not exceeding 60 days or to a fine not exceeding level 3 on the standard scale or both.

(2) Any person who—

(a) is in possession of alcohol in; or

(b) while in possession of alcohol, attempts to enter, the relevant area of a designated sports ground at any time during the period of a designated sporting event, shall be guilty of an offence and liable on summary conviction to imprisonment for a period not exceeding 60 days or to a fine not exceeding level 3 on the standard scale or both.

(3) Any person who has entered the relevant area of a designated sports ground and is in possession of a controlled article or substance at any time during the period of a designated sporting event shall be guilty of an offence.

(4) Any person who, while in possession of a controlled article or substance, attempts to enter the relevant area of a designated sports ground at any time during the period of a designated sporting event at the ground shall be guilty of an offence.

(5) A person guilty of an offence under subsection (3) or (4) above shall be liable on summary conviction to imprisonment for a period not exceeding 60 days or to a fine not exceeding level 3 on the standard scale or both.

(6) It shall be a defence for a person charged with an offence under subsection (3) or (4) above to show that he had been lawful authority to be in possession of the controlled article or substance.

(7) Any person who—

(a) is drunk in; or

(b) while drunk, attempts to enter, the relevant area of a designated sports ground at any time during the period of a designated sporting event shall be guilty of an offence and liable on summary conviction to a fine not exceeding level 2 on the standard scale.

(8) In this section—

"controlled article or substance" means—

(a) any article or substance whose main purpose is the emission of a flare for purposes of illuminating or signalling (as opposed to igniting or heating) or the emission of smoke or a visible gas; and in particular it includes distress flares, fog signals, and pellets and capsules intended to be used as fumigators or for testing pipes, but not matches, cigarette lighters or heaters; and

(b) any article which is a firework.

"controlled container" means any bottle, can or other portable container, whether open or sealed, which is, or was, in its original manufactured state, capable of containing liquid and is made from such material or is of such construction, or is so adapted, that if it were thrown at or propelled against a person it would be capable of causing some injury to that person; but the term does not include a container holding a medicinal product for a medicinal purpose.

"medicinal product" and "medicinal purpose" have the meanings assigned to those terms by section 130 of the Medicines Act 1968.

DEFINITIONS

"controlled article or substance": subs.(8).
"controlled container": subs.(8).
"relevant area": s.23.

GENERAL NOTE

This section provides for offences of being in possession of a controlled container, alcohol, controlled article or substance or being drunk, while in or attempting to enter, the relevant area of a designated sports ground. The definition of controlled articles, substances and containers covers items which would be likely to cause injury to a person. There is a defence of "lawful authority" in subs.(7).

Police powers of enforcement

21. For the purpose of enforcing the provisions of this Part of this Act, a constable shall have the power without warrant—

(a) to enter a designated sports ground at any time during the period of a designated sporting event;

(b) to search a person who he has reasonable grounds to suspect is committing or has committed an offence under this Part of this Act;

(c) to stop and search a vehicle where he has reasonable grounds to suspect that an offence under section 19 of this Act is being or has been committed;

(d) to arrest a person who he has reasonable grounds to suspect is committing or has committed an offence under this Part of this Act;

(e) to seize and detain—

(i) with its contents (if any), a controlled container as defined in section 20(8) of this Act, or

    (ii) with its contents, any other container if he has reasonable grounds to suspect that those contents are or include alcohol; or

    (iii) a controlled article or substance as defined in section 20(8) of this Act.

AMENDMENT

Subs.(e)(iii) inserted by the Crime and Punishment (Scotland) Act 1997 (c.48), s.62(1) and Sch.1, para.18(5); brought into force by the Crime and Punishment (Scotland) Act 1997 (Commencement and Transitional Provisions) Order 1997 (SI 1997/1712), para.3 (August 1, 1997).

GENERAL NOTE

This section contains the powers of the police to employ the provisions of this Part of the Act. The 1997 Act extends the power of seizure to include flares and fireworks which, anomolously, had not been included in the original statute. Apart from the power to enter a designated sports ground the use of the powers require the constable to have "reasonable grounds to suspect"—an objective test which if not met will render the use of the powers unlawful and any evidence recovered as a result thereof inadmissible.

Presumption as to contents of container

22. Section 127 of the Licensing (Scotland) Act 1976 (presumption as to contents of container) shall apply for the purposes of any trial in connection with an alleged contravention of any provision of this Part of this Act as it applies for the purposes of any trial in connection with an alleged contravention of any provision of that Act.

GENERAL NOTE

The most important provisions in s.127 of the Licensing (Scotland) Act 1976 for the purposes of this section are that any liquid found in a container which is sealed or open, shall be presumed to conform to the description of the liquid on the container. No notice is required of the prosecutor's intention to rely on the presumption since the Law Reform (Miscellaneous Provisions) (Scotland) Act 1990, but the defence may lead evidence to rebut the presumption if they give seven days notice of their intention to do so to the prosecutor.

The definition of "alcohol" in s.139(1) of the Licensing (Scotland) Act 1976, at that time did not include "any liquor which ... is found to be of an original gravity not exceeding 1016 degrees and to be of a strength not exceeding 2 degrees of proof ...". Where therefore the Crown sought to rely on the presumption where the objects in question were bottles of cider which were labelled as "strong cider fermented to full strength" but gave no indication of gravity or strength of the liquid, there was insufficient evidence that what was in the bottles was "alcohol": *Tudhope v McDonald*, 1986 S.C.C.R. 32; see also *Grieve v Hamilton*, 1987 S.C.C.R. 317. The present definition provides for exclusion by reference to strength—not exceeding 0.5 per cent of ethyl alcohol by volume (at a temperature of 20 degrees celsius): see *Davenport v Wilson*, High Court of Justiciary, November 1, 1994, Crown Office Circular A5/95, where the label in question read "Grant's Vodka 35cl 37.5% vol". The court held that the label indicated that the bottle contained 37.5 per cent of something by volume and the description of the contents as vodka led to the obvious conclusion that the words related to the alcoholic content of the liquor inside the bottle.

Interpretation of Part II

23. In this Part of this Act, unless the context otherwise requires—

    "advertised" means announced in any written or printed document or in any broadcast announcement;

    "alcohol" means alcoholic liquor as defined in section 139 of the Licensing (Scotland) Act 1976;

    "designated" means designated by the Secretary of State by order under section 18 of this Act, and "designated sporting event" includes a

sporting event designated under section 9(3)(a) of the Sporting
Events (Control of Alcohol) Etc. Act 1985;
"keeper", in relation to a vehicle, means the person having the duty to
take out a licence for it under section 1(1) of the Vehicles Excise
and Registration Act 1994;
"motor vehicle" means a mechanically propelled vehicle intended or
adapted for use on roads;
"period of a designated sporting event" means the period commencing
two hours before the start and ending one hour after the end of a
designated sporting event, except that where the event is advertised
as to start at a particular time but is delayed or postponed in includes, and where for any reason an event does not take place it
means, the period commencing two hours before and ending one
hour after, that particular time;
"public service vehicle" has the same meaning as in the Public Passenger
Vehicles Act 1981 and "operator" in relation to such a vehicle
means—
    (a)   the driver if he owns the vehicle; and
    (b)   in any case the person for whom the driver works (whether un-
          der a contract of employment or any other description of
          contract personally to do work);
"railway passenger vehicle" has the same meaning as in the Licensing
(Scotland) Act 1976;
"relevant area" means any part of a sports ground—
    (a)   to which spectators attending a designated sporting event are
          granted access on payment; or
    (b)   from which a designated sporting event may be viewed directly;
"sporting event" means any physical competitive activity at a sports
ground, and includes any such activity which has been advertised as
to, but does not, take place; and
"sports ground" means any place whatsoever which is designed, or is capable of being adapted, for the holding of sporting events in respect of
which spectators are accommodated.

AMENDMENT

Section 23 as amended by the Crime and Punishment (Scotland) Act 1997 (c.48), s.62(1) and
Sch.1, para.18(6); brought into force by the Crime and Punishment (Scotland) Act 1997 (Commencement and Transitional Provisions) Order 1997 (SI 1997/1712), para.3 (August 1, 1997).

CRIMINAL PROCEDURE (SCOTLAND) ACT 1995

(1995 c.46)

An Act to consolidate certain enactments relating to criminal procedure in Scotland

[8th November 1995]

. . .

Sufficient evidence

Evidence as to controlled drugs and medicinal products

282. —(1) [1] For the purposes of any criminal proceedings, evidence given by an authorised forensic scientist, either orally or in a report purporting to be signed by him, that a substance which satisfies either of the conditions specified in subsection (2) below is—

(a) a particular controlled drug or medicinal product; or

(b) a particular product which is listed in the British Pharmacopoeia as containing a particular controlled drug or medicinal product,

shall, subject to subsection (3) below, be sufficient evidence of that fact notwithstanding that no analysis of the substance has been carried out.

(2) Those conditions are—

(a) that the substance is in a sealed container bearing a label identifying the contents of the container; or

(b) that the substance has a characteristic appearance having regard to its size, shape, colour and manufacturer's mark.

(3) A party proposing to rely on subsection (1) above ("the first party") shall, not less than 14 days before the trial diet, serve on the other party ("the second party")—

(a) a notice to that effect; and

(b) where the evidence is contained in a report, a copy of the report, and if the second party serves on the first party, not more than seven days after the date of service of the notice on him, a notice that he does not accept the evidence as to the identity of the substance, subsection (1) above shall not apply in relation to that evidence.

(4) A notice or copy report served in accordance with subsection (3) above shall be served in such manner as may be prescribed by Act of Adjournal; and a written execution purporting to be signed by the person who served the notice or copy together with, where appropriate, the relevant post office receipt shall be sufficient evidence of such service.

(5) In this section—

"controlled drug" has the same meaning as in the Misuse of Drugs Act 1971; and

"medicinal product" has the same meaning as in the Medicines Act 1968.

DEFINITIONS

"controlled drug": s.282(5) and s.2(1)(a) of the Misuse of Drugs Act 1971 (c.38).
"medicinal product": s.282(5) and s.130(1) of the Medicines Act 1968 (c.67).

---

[1] *Annotation by Iain Bradley and Robert Shiels, Solicitors.*

"trial": s.307(1).

GENERAL NOTE

This section, introduced by the Criminal Justice (Scotland) Act 1995, s.25, enables evidence to be given, in certain circumstances, by an authorised forensic scientist in any criminal proceedings to the effect that a substance is listed in British Pharmacopoiea as being, or containing, a controlled drug or medicinal product. Instead of demanding the conduct of a chemical examination to establish identification, s.282 allows forensic identification to be achieved by reference either to the label on a sealed container or, as is more common, to the size, colour, shape and markings on the substance; this latter method is commonplace in medical practice and in the pharmaceutical industry and there seems little virtue in requiring a higher standard than that in criminal proceedings particularly when subs.(3)(b) preserves the rights of the other party to give formal notice of challenge to that evidence.

Any such forensic report can be served in accordance with subs.(3) not less than 14 days prior to trial may broadly follow the style of Form 27, and must be challenged within seven days of the date of service, not receipt. Such a report must be served on all other parties in the proceedings.

. . .

TOBACCO ADVERTISING AND PROMOTION ACT 2002

(2002 c.36)

ARRANGEMENT OF SECTIONS

An Act to control the advertising and promotion of tobacco products; and for connected purposes.

[7th November 2002]

Meaning of "tobacco advertisement" and "tobacco product"

1. In this Act—
   "tobacco advertisement" means an advertisement—
       (a)   whose purpose is to promote a tobacco product, or
       (b)   whose effect is to do so, and
   "tobacco product" means a product consisting wholly or partly of tobacco and intended to be smoked, sniffed, sucked or chewed.

Prohibition of tobacco advertising

2. — (1) A person who in the course of a business publishes a tobacco advertisement, or causes one to be published, in the United Kingdom is guilty of an offence.

(2) A person who in the course of a business prints, devises or distributes in the United Kingdom a tobacco advertisement which is published in the United Kingdom, or causes such a tobacco advertisement to be so printed, devised or distributed, is guilty of an offence.

(3) Distributing a tobacco advertisement includes transmitting it in electronic form, participating in doing so, and providing the means of transmission.

(4) It is not an offence under subsection (1) for a person who does not

67

carry on business in the United Kingdom to publish or cause to be published a tobacco advertisement by means of a website which is accessed in the United Kingdom; and, in that case, devising the advertisement or causing it to be devised is not an offence under subsection (2).

Advertising: newspapers, periodicals etc

3. If a newspaper, periodical or other publication ("the publication") containing a tobacco advertisement is in the course of a business published in the United Kingdom—
- (a) any proprietor or editor of the publication is guilty of an offence,
- (b) any person who (directly or indirectly) procured the inclusion of the advertisement in the publication is guilty of an offence, and
- (c) any person who sells the publication, or offers it for sale, or otherwise makes it available to the public, is guilty of an offence.

Advertising: exclusions

4. — (1) No offence is committed under section 2 or 3 in relation to a tobacco advertisement—
- (a) if it is, or is contained in, a communication made in the course of a business which is part of the tobacco trade, and for the purposes of that trade, and directed solely at persons who—
    - (i) are engaged in, or employed by, a business which is also part of that trade, and
    - (ii) fall within subsection (2),
    in their capacity as such persons,
- (b) if it is, or is contained in, the communication made in reply to a particular request by an individual for information about a tobacco product, or
- (c) if it is contained in a publication (other than an in-flight magazine) whose principal market is not the United Kingdom (or any part of it), or if it is contained in any internet version of such a publication.
- (2) A person falls within this subsection if—
- (a) he is responsible for making decisions on behalf of the business referred to in subsection (1)(a)(i) about the purchase of tobacco products which are to be sold in the course of that business,
- (b) he occupies a position in the management structure of the business in question which is equivalent in seniority to, or of greater seniority than, that of any such person, or
- (c) he is the person who, or is a member of the board of directors or other body of persons (however described) which, is responsible for the conduct of the business in question.
- (3) The appropriate Minister may provide in regulations that no offence is committed under section 2 in relation to a tobacco advertisement which—
- (a) is in a place or on a website where tobacco products are offered for sale, and
- (b) complies with requirements specified in the regulations.
- (4) The regulations may, in particular, provide for the meaning of "place" in subsection (3)(a).

Advertising: defences

5. — (1) A person does not commit an offence under section 2 or section 3(a) or (b), in connection with an advertisement whose purpose is to promote a tobacco product, if he did not know, and had no reason to suspect, that the purpose of the advertisement was to promote a tobacco product.

(2) A person does not commit such an offence in connection with an advertisement whose effect is to promote a tobacco product if he could not reasonably have foreseen that that would be the effect of the advertisement.

(3) A person does not commit an offence under section 2(2) or 3(a) or (b) if he did not know, and had no reason to suspect, that the tobacco advertisement would be published in the United Kingdom.

(4) A person does not commit an offence under section 2(2) of distributing or causing the distribution of a tobacco advertisement, otherwise than as mentioned in section 2(3), if he did not know, and had no reason to suspect, that what he distributed or caused to be distributed was, or contained, a tobacco advertisement.

(5) In relation to a tobacco advertisement which is distributed as mentioned in section 2(3), a person does not commit an offence under section 2(2) of distributing it or causing its distribution if—

(a) he was unaware that what he distributed or caused to be distributed was, or contained, a tobacco advertisement,

(b) having become aware of it, it was not reasonably practicable for him to prevent its further distribution, or

(c) he did not carry on business in the United Kingdom at the relevant time.

(6) A person does not commit an offence under section 3(c) if he did not know, and had no reason to suspect, that the publication contained a tobacco advertisement.

Specialist tobacconists

6. —(1) A person does not commit an offence under section 2 if the tobacco advertisement—

(a) was in, or fixed to the outside of the premises of, a specialist tobacconist,

(b) was not for cigarettes or hand-rolling tobacco, and

(c) complied with any requirements specified by the appropriate Minister in regulations in relation to tobacco advertisements on the premises of specialist tobacconists.

(2) A specialist tobacconist is a shop selling tobacco products by retail (whether or not it also sells other things) more than half of whose sales on the premises in question derive from the sale of cigars, snuff, pipe tobacco and smoking accessories.

(3) The sales referred to in subsection (2) are to be measured by sale price—

(a) during the most recent period of twelve months for which accounts are available, or

(b) during the period for which the shop has been established, if it has not been established long enough for twelve months' accounts to be available.

(4) "Shop", in subsections (2) and (3), includes a self-contained part of a shop; and, in that case, "premises" in subsections (1) and (2) means that self-contained part of the shop.

Developments in technology

7. The Secretary of State may by order amend any provision of this Act if he considers it appropriate to do so in consequence of any developments in technology relating to publishing or distributing by electronic means.

Displays

8. —(1) A person who in the course of a business displays or causes to be displayed tobacco products or their prices in a place or on a website where tobacco products are offered for sale is guilty of an offence if the display does not comply with such requirements (if any) as may be specified by the appropriate Minister in regulations.

(2) It is not an offence under subsection (1) for a person who does not carry on business in the United Kingdom to display or cause to be displayed tobacco products or their prices by means of a website which is accessed in the United Kingdom.

(3) The regulations may, in particular, provide for the meaning of "place" in subsection (1).

(4) The regulations must make provision for a display which also amounts to an advertisement to be treated for the purpose of offences under this Act—

(a)   as an advertisement and not as a display, or

(b)   as a display and not as an advertisement.

Prohibition of free distributions

9. —(1) A person is guilty of an offence if in the course of a business he—

(a)   gives any product or coupon away to the public in the United Kingdom, or

(b)   causes or permits that to happen,

and the purpose or effect of giving the product or coupon away is to promote a tobacco product.

(2) It does not matter whether the product or coupon accompanies something else, or is given away separately.

(3) No offence is committed under subsection (1) if—

(a)   the business referred to in subsection (1) is part of the tobacco trade,

(b)   the product or coupon is given away for the purposes of that trade,

(c)   each person to whom it is given—

(i)   is engaged in, or employed by, a business which is also part of the tobacco trade, and

(ii)   falls within subsection (4), and

(d)   the product or coupon is given to each such person in his capacity as such a person.

(4) A person falls within this subsection if—

(a)   he is responsible for making decisions on behalf of the business referred to in subsection (3)(c)(i) about the purchase of tobacco products which are to be sold in the course of that business,

(b)   he occupies a position in the management structure of the business in question which is equivalent in seniority to, or of greater seniority than, that of any such person, or

(c)   he is the person who, or is a member of the board of directors or other body of persons (however described) which, is responsible for the conduct of the business in question.

(5) A person does not commit an offence under this section—

(a)   where it is alleged that the purpose of giving the product or coupon away was to promote a tobacco product, if he did not know and had no reason to suspect that that was its purpose, or

(b)   where it is alleged that the effect of giving the product or coupon away was to promote a tobacco product, if he could not reasonably have foreseen that that would be its effect.

(6) "Coupon" means a document or other thing which (whether by itself or not) can be redeemed for a product or service or for cash or any other benefit.

(7) The Secretary of State may make regulations providing for this section to apply to making products or coupons available for a nominal sum or at a substantial discount as it applies to giving them away.

(8) If regulations under subsection (7) provide for this section to apply to making products or coupons available at a substantial discount, the regulations must provide for the meaning of "substantial discount".

(9) The regulations may provide that this section is to apply in that case with such modifications (if any) specified in the regulations as the Secretary of State considers appropriate.

Prohibition of sponsorship

10. —(1) A person who is party to a sponsorship agreement is guilty of an offence if the purpose or effect of anything done as a result of the agreement is to promote a tobacco product in the United Kingdom.

(2) A sponsorship agreement is an agreement under which, in the course of a business, a party to it makes a contribution towards something, whether the contribution is in money or takes any other form (for example, the provision of services or of contributions in kind).

(3) A person does not commit an offence under this section—

(a) where it is alleged that the purpose of what was done as a result of the agreement was to promote a tobacco product in the United Kingdom, if he did not know, and had no reason to suspect, that that was its purpose, or

(b) where it is alleged that the effect of what was done as a result of the agreement was to promote a tobacco product in the United Kingdom, if he could not reasonably have foreseen that that would be its effect.

(4) A person does not commit an offence under this section if he did not know and had no reason to suspect that the contribution referred to in subsection (2) was made in the course of a business.

Brandsharing

11. —(1) The Secretary of State may by regulations make provision prohibiting or restricting, in such circumstances and subject to such exceptions as may be specified in the regulations, the use—

(a) in connection with any service or product (other than a tobacco product), of any name, emblem or other feature of a description specified in the regulations which is the same as, or similar to, a name, emblem or other feature so specified which is connected with a tobacco product, or

(b) in connection with any tobacco product, of any name, emblem or other feature of a description specified in the regulations which is the same as, or similar to, a name, emblem or other feature so specified which is connected with any service or product other than a tobacco product.

(2) Provision made by virtue of subsection (1) may prohibit or restrict only that use whose purpose is to promote a tobacco product, or whose effect is to do so.

(3) If regulations under this section provide for a prohibition or restriction to be subject to an exception, the regulations may also make such provision as the Secretary of State considers appropriate for a corresponding exception to have effect for the purposes of offences under section 2, 3, 8, 9 or 10.

(4) A person who contravenes a prohibition or restriction contained in regulations made under this section is guilty of an offence.

Television and radio broadcasting

12. — (1) In this section "the 1990 Act" means the Broadcasting Act 1990 (c.42) and "the 1996 Act" means the Broadcasting Act 1996 (c.55).

(2) This Act does not apply in relation to anything included in a service to which any of subsections (3) to (6) apply.

(3) This subsection applies to a service which—

(a) falls within section 2(1) of the 1990 Act (television services, etc regulated under Part 1 of the 1990 Act or Part 1 of the 1996 Act), and

(b) is not an additional service within the meaning of section 48(1) of the 1990 Act other than a teletext service.

(4) This subsection applies to a local delivery service within the meaning of section 72 of the 1990 Act.

(5) This subsection applies to a service falling within section 84 of the 1990 Act (independent radio services regulated under Part 3 of the 1990 Act or Part 2 of the 1996 Act) other than a digital additional service within the meaning of section 63(1) of the 1996 Act.

(6) This subsection applies to a service provided by the British Broadcasting Corporation or Sianel Pedwar Cymru (the Welsh Authority referred to in section 56 of the 1990 Act).

Enforcement

13. — (1) For the purposes of this Act "enforcement authority" means—

(a) in England and Wales, a weights and measures authority,

(b) in Scotland, a local weights and measures authority, and

(c) in Northern Ireland, a district council.

(2) It is the duty of an enforcement authority to enforce within its area the provisions of this Act and regulations made under it.

(3) The appropriate Minister may direct, in relation to cases of a particular description or a particular case, that any duty imposed on an enforcement authority in England and Wales or Scotland by subsection (2) shall be discharged by the appropriate Minister and not by the enforcement authority.

(4) The Department of Health, Social Services and Public Safety may direct, in relation to cases of a particular description or a particular case, that any duty imposed on an enforcement authority in Northern Ireland by subsection (2) shall be discharged by the Department and not by the enforcement authority.

(5) The Secretary of State may take over the conduct of any proceedings instituted in England and Wales by another person under any provision of this Act or regulations made under it.

(6) The Department of Health, Social Services and Public Safety may take over the conduct of any proceedings instituted in Northern Ireland by another person under any provision of this Act or regulations made under it.

(7) For the purposes of the trying of offences under this Act or regulations made under it—

(a) any such offence committed in England or Wales may be treated as having been committed in any place in England or Wales, so that any magistrates' court in England or Wales has jurisdiction to try the offence, and

(b) any such offence committed in Northern Ireland may be treated as having been committed in any place in Northern Ireland, so that any magistrates' court in Northern Ireland has jurisdiction to hear and determine a complaint charging the offence.

Powers of entry, etc

14. —(1) A duly authorised officer of an enforcement authority has the right, on producing, if so required, his written authority—

(a) at any reasonable hour to enter any premises, other than premises used only as a private dwelling house, which he considers it is necessary for him to enter for the purpose of the proper exercise of his functions under this Act,

(b) to carry out on those premises such inspections and examinations as he considers necessary for that purpose,

(c) where he considers it necessary for that purpose, to require the production of any book, document, data, record (in whatever form it is held) or product and inspect it, and take copies of or extracts from it,

(d) to take possession of any book, document, data, record (in whatever form it is held) or product which is on the premises and retain it for as long as he considers necessary for that purpose,

(e) to require any person to give him such information, or afford him such facilities and assistance, as he considers necessary for that purpose.

(2) A duly authorised officer of an enforcement authority may make such purchases and secure the provision of such services as he considers necessary for the purpose of the proper exercise of his functions under this Act.

(3) A person is not obliged by subsection (1) to answer any question or produce any document which he would be entitled to refuse to answer or to produce—

(a) in or for the purposes of proceedings in a court in England and Wales, where the question is asked or the document is required by a duly authorised officer of an enforcement authority in England and Wales,

(b) in or for the purposes of proceedings in a court in Northern Ireland, where the question is asked or the document is required by a duly authorised officer of an enforcement authority in Northern Ireland,

(c) in or for the purposes of proceedings in a court in Scotland, where the question is asked or the document is required by a duly authorised officer of an enforcement authority in Scotland.

(4) If a justice of the peace is satisfied by any written information on oath that for the purpose of the proper exercise of the functions of an enforcement authority under this Act there are reasonable grounds for entry into any premises, other than premises used only as a private dwelling house, and—

(a) that admission to the premises has been or is likely to be refused and that notice of intention to apply for a warrant under this subsection has been given to the occupier, or

(b) that an application for admission, or the giving of such notice, would defeat the object of the entry or that the premises are unoccupied or that the occupier is temporarily absent and it might defeat the object of the entry to await his return,

the justice may by warrant signed by him, which shall continue in force until the end of the period of one month beginning with the date on which he signs it, authorise any duly authorised officer of an enforcement authority to enter the premises, if need be by force.

(5) A duly authorised officer entering any premises by virtue of subsection (1) or of a warrant under subsection (4) may take with him when he enters those premises such other persons and such equipment as he considers necessary.

(6) On leaving any premises which a duly authorised officer is authorised to enter by a warrant under subsection (4), that officer shall, if the premises are unoccupied or the occupier is temporarily absent, leave the premises as effectively secured against trespassers as he found them.

(7) Where by virtue of subsection (1)(d) a duly authorised officer takes

possession of any item, he shall leave on the premises from which the item was removed a statement giving particulars of what he has taken and stating that he has taken possession of it.

(8)   In the application of this section to Northern Ireland, the reference in subsection (4) to any information on oath shall be construed as a reference to any complaint on oath.

(9)   In the application of this section to Scotland, the reference in subsection (4) to a justice of the peace shall be construed as a reference to a sheriff.

(10)   Where a direction of the appropriate Minister has effect under section 13(3), this section and section 15 have effect, in relation to any case or case of a description specified in the direction, as if references to a duly authorised officer of an enforcement authority were references to a person acting on behalf of the appropriate Minister.

(11)   Where a direction of the Department of Health, Social Services and Public Safety has effect under section 13(4), this section and section 15 have effect, in relation to any case or case of a description specified in the direction, as if references to a duly authorised officer of an enforcement authority were references to a person acting on behalf of the Department.

(12)   Where—
(a)   the Secretary of State takes over any proceedings by virtue of section 13(5), or
(b)   the Department of Health, Social Services and Public Safety takes over the conduct of any proceedings by virtue of section 13(6),
this section and section 15 have effect, in relation to any case which is the subject of such proceedings, as if references to a duly authorised officer of an enforcement authority were references to a person acting on behalf of the Secretary of State or (as the case may be) the Department.

Obstruction, etc of officers

15. —(1) A person who—
(a)   intentionally obstructs a duly authorised officer of an enforcement authority who is acting in the proper exercise of his functions under this Act, or
(b)   without reasonable cause fails to comply with any requirement made of him by such an officer who is so acting,
is guilty of an offence.

(2)   A person who, in giving any information which is properly required of him by a duly authorised officer of an enforcement authority, makes a statement which is false in a material particular is guilty of an offence.

(3)   A person does not commit an offence under subsection (2) if—
(a)   he did not know the material particular was false, and
(b)   he had reasonable grounds to believe that it was true.

Penalties

16. —(1) A person guilty of an offence under section 15(1) is liable on summary conviction to a fine not exceeding level 3 on the standard scale.

(2)   A person guilty of an offence under or by virtue of any other provision of this Act is liable—
(a)   on summary conviction to imprisonment for a term not exceeding six months, or a fine not exceeding level 5 on the standard scale, or both, or
(b)   on conviction on indictment to imprisonment for a term not exceeding 2 years, or a fine, or both.

Defences: burden of proof

17. —(1) This section applies where a person charged with an offence under this Act relies on a defence under any of sections 5(1) to (6), 6(1), 9(5), 10(3) and (4) and 15(3).

(2) Where evidence is adduced which is sufficient to raise an issue with respect to that defence, the court or jury shall assume that the defence is satisfied unless the prosecution proves beyond reasonable doubt that it is not.

Offences by bodies corporate and Scottish partnerships

18. —(1) If an offence under any provision of this Act committed by a body corporate is proved—

(a) to have been committed with the consent or connivance of an officer, or

(b) to be attributable to any neglect on his part,

the officer as well as the body corporate is guilty of the offence and liable to be proceeded against and punished accordingly.

(2) In subsection (1) "officer", in relation to a body corporate, means a director, manager, secretary or other similar officer of the body, or a person purporting to act in any such capacity.

(3) If the affairs of a body corporate are managed by its members, subsection (1) applies in relation to the acts and defaults of a member in connection with his functions of management as if he were a director of the body corporate.

(4) If an offence under any provision of this Act committed by a partnership in Scotland is proved—

(a) to have been committed with the consent or connivance of a partner, or

(b) to be attributable to any neglect on his part,

the partner as well as the partnership is guilty of the offence and liable to be proceeded against and punished accordingly.

(5) In subsection (4) "partner" includes a person purporting to act as a partner.

Regulations

19. —(1) Powers to make regulations and orders under this Act are exercisable by statutory instrument.

(2) Regulations, and orders under section 7, may make—

(a) different provision for different cases or circumstances, and

(b) any supplementary, consequential or transitional provision which the appropriate Minister (or the Secretary of State) considers necessary or desirable.

(3) No statutory instrument containing an order under section 7 or regulations under section 9 or 11 is to be made unless a draft of the instrument has been laid before Parliament and approved by a resolution of each House of Parliament.

(4) No statutory instrument containing regulations under section 8 is to be made unless a draft of the instrument has been laid before Parliament and approved by a resolution of each House of Parliament, or laid before the Scottish Parliament and approved by a resolution of that Parliament.

(5) A statutory instrument containing regulations under any other provision of this Act shall be subject to annulment in pursuance of a resolution of either House of Parliament or of the Scottish Parliament.

Transitional provisions: sponsorship

20. — (1) The appropriate Minister may make regulations providing that, subject to the satisfaction (or continuing satisfaction) of any conditions specified in the regulations, section 10 is not to apply before a date so specified to a sponsorship agreement of a description so specified.

(2) The date specified may not be later than 1st October 2006.

(3) If, by virtue of regulations under this section, section 10 does not apply to a sponsorship agreement, the doing of anything as a result of that agreement is not an offence under any provision of this Act.

Interpretation

21. In this Act—

"appropriate Minister" means —

    (a)   in relation to England, Wales and Northern Ireland, the Secretary of State, and

    (b)   in relation to Scotland, the Scottish Ministers,

"public" means the public generally, any section of the public or individually selected members of the public,

"purpose" includes one of a number of purposes, and

"tobacco advertisement" and "tobacco product" have the meaning given in section 1,

and references to publishing include any means of publishing (and include, in particular, publishing by any electronic means, for example by means of the internet).

Commencement, short title and extent

22. — (1) Apart from this section, this Act comes into force on such day as the appropriate Minister may by order appoint.

(2) Different days may be appointed under subsection (1) for different provisions and for different purposes.

(3) Such an order may include such transitional provisions and savings as the appropriate Minister considers appropriate.

(4) This Act may be cited as the Tobacco Advertising and Promotion Act 2002.

(5) This Act extends to Northern Ireland.

MISUSE OF DRUGS REGULATIONS 1985

(SI 1985 No. 2066)

(December 19, 1985)

ARRANGEMENT OF SECTIONS

In pursuance of sections 7, 10, 22 and 31 of the Misuse of Drugs Act 1971 after consultation with the Advisory Council on the Misuse of Drugs, I hereby make the following Regulations:—

Citation and commencement

1. These Regulations may be cited as the Misuse of Drugs Regulations 1985 and shall come into operation on 1st April 1986.

Interpretation

2. —(1) In these Regulations, unless the context otherwise requires, the expression—

"the Act" means the Misuse of Drugs Act 1971;

"authorised as a member of a group" means authorised by virtue of being a member of a class as respects which the Secretary of State has granted an authority under and for the purposes of Regulations 8(3), 9(3) or 10(3) which is in force, and "his group authority", in relation to a person who is a member of such a class, means the authority so granted to that class;

"document" has the same meaning as in Part I of the Civil Evidence Act 1968;

"exempt product" means a preparation or other product consisting of one or more components parts, any of which contains a controlled drug, where—

    (a)   the preparation or other product is not designed for administration of the controlled drug to a human being or animal;

    (b)   the controlled drug in any component part is packaged in such a form, or in combination with other active or inert substances in such a manner, that it cannot be recovered by readily applicable means or in yield which constitutes a risk to health; and

    (c)   no one component part of the product or preparation contains more than one milligram of the controlled drug or one microgram in the case of lysergide or any other N-alkyl derivative of lysergamide;

"health prescription" means a prescription issued by a doctor or a dentist either under the National Health Service Act 1977, the National Health Service (Scotland) Act, 1978, or a form issued by a local authority for use in connection with the health service of that authority;

"installation manager" and "offshore installation" have the same meanings as in the Mineral Workings (Offshore Installations) Act 1971;

"master" and "seamen" have the same meanings as in the Merchant Shipping Act 1894;

"medicinal product" has the same meaning as in the Medicines Act 1968;

"the Merchant Shipping Acts" means the Merchant Shipping Acts 1894 to 1984;

"officer of customs and excise" means an officer within the meaning of the Customs and Excise Management Act 1979;

"prescription" means a prescription issued by a doctor for the medical treatment of a single individual, by a dentist for the dental treatment of a single individual or by a veterinary surgeon or veterinary practitioner for the purposes of animal treatment;

"register" means a bound book and does not include any form of loose leaf register or card index;

"registered pharmacy" has the same meaning as in the Medicines Act 1968;

"retail dealer" means a person lawfully conducting a retail pharmacy business or a pharmacist engaged in supplying drugs to the public at a health centre within the meaning of the Medicines Act 1968;

"sister or acting sister" includes any male nurse occupying a similar position;

"wholesale dealer" means a person who carries on the business of selling drugs to persons who buy to sell again.

(2) In these Regulations any reference to a Regulation or Schedule shall be construed as a reference to a Regulation contained in these Regulations or, as the case may be, to a Schedule thereto; and any reference in a Regulation or Schedule to a paragraph shall be construed as a reference to a paragraph of that Regulation or Schedule.

(3) Nothing in these Regulations shall be construed as derogating from any power or immunity of the Crown, its servants or agents.

AMENDMENT

Reg.2 as amended by the Misuse of Drugs (Amendment) Regulations 1999 (SI 1999/1404) reg.2(2) (effective July 1, 1999).

Specification of Controlled Drugs for Purposes of Regulations

3. Schedules 1 to 5 shall have effect for the purpose of specifying the controlled drugs to which certain provisions of these Regulations apply.

Exceptions for Drugs in Schedules 4 and 5 and Poppy-straw

4. — (1) Section 3(1) of the Act (which prohibits the importation and exportation of controlled drugs) shall not have effect in relation to the drugs specified in Part II of Schedule 4 and Schedule 5.

(1A) The application of section 3(1) of the Act in so far as it creates an offence and of sections 50(1) to (4), 68(2) and (3) or 170 of the Customs and Excise Management Act 1979 in so far as they apply in relation to a prohibition or restriction on importation or exportation having effect by virtue of section 3 of the Act, are hereby excluded in the case of importation or exportation by any person for administration to himself of any drug specified in Part I of Schedule 4 which is contained in a medicinal product.

(2) Section 5(1) of the Act (which prohibits the possession of controlled drugs) shall not have effect in relation to—

(a) any drug specified in Schedule 4 which is contained in a medicinal product;

(b) the drugs specified in Schedule 5.

(3) Sections 4(1) (which prohibits the production and supply of controlled drugs) and 5(1) of the Act shall not have effect in relation to poppy-straw.

(4) Sections 3(1), 4(1) and 5(1) of the Act shall not have effect in relation to any exempt product.

AMENDMENTS

Subs.(1) as amended by the Misuse of Drugs (Amendment) Regulations 1996 (SI 1996/1597) reg.2(3).

Subs.(1A) inserted by reg.2(4) of the above Regulations.

Subs.(4) inserted by the Misuse of Drugs (Amendment) Regulations 1999 (SI 1999/1404) reg.2(3) (effective July 1, 1999).

Licences to Produce etc. Controlled Drugs

5. Where any person is authorised by a licence of the Secretary of State issued under this Regulation and for the time being in force to produce, supply, offer to supply or have in his possession any controlled drug, it shall not by virtue of Section 4(1) or 5(1) of the Act be unlawful for that person to produce, supply, offer to supply or have in his possession that drug in accordance with the terms of the licence and in compliance with any conditions attached to the licence.

General Authority to Supply and Possess

6. — (1) Notwithstanding the provisions of Section 4(1)(b) of the Act, any person who is lawfully in possession of a controlled drug may supply that drug to the person from whom he obtained it.

(2) Notwithstanding the provisions of Section 4(1)(b) of the Act, any person who has in his possession a drug specified in Schedule 2, 3, 4 or 5 which has been supplied by or on the prescription of a practitioner for the treatment of that person, or of a person whom he represents, may supply that drug to any doctor, dentist or pharmacist for the purpose of destruction.

(3) Notwithstanding the provisions of Section 4(1)(b) of the Act, any person who is lawfully in possession of a drug specified in Schedule 2, 3, 4 or 5 which has been supplied by or on the prescription of a veterinary practitioner or veterinary surgeon for the treatment of animals may supply that drug to any veterinary practitioner, veterinary surgeon or pharmacist for the purpose of destruction.

(4) It shall not by virtue of Section 4(1)(b) or 5(1) of the Act be unlawful for any person in respect of whom a licence has been granted and is in force under Section 16(1) of the Wildlife and Countryside Act 1981 to supply, offer to supply or have in his possession any drug specified in Schedule 2 or 3 for the purposes for which that licence was granted.

(5) Notwithstanding the provisions of Section 4(1)(b) of the Act, any of the persons specified in paragraph (7) may supply any controlled drug to any person who may lawfully have that drug in his possession.

(6) Notwithstanding the provisions of Section 5(1) of the Act, any of the persons so specified may have any controlled drug in his possession.

(7) The persons referred to in paragraphs (5) and (6) are—

(a) a constable when acting in the course of his duty as such;

(b) a person engaged in the business of a carrier when acting in the course of that business;

(c) a person engaged in the business of a postal operator (within the meaning of the Postal Services Act 2000) when acting in the course of that business;

(d) an officer of customs and excise when acting in the course of his duty as such;

(e) a person engaged in the work of any laboratory to which the drug has been sent for forensic examination when acting in the course of his duty as a person so engaged;

(f) a person engaged in conveying the drug to a person who may lawfully have that drug in his possession.

AMENDMENTS

Subs.(4) as amended by the Misuse of Drugs (Amendment) Regulations 1988 (SI 1988/916) reg.2(2).

Subs.(7)(c) as amended by the Postal Services Act 2000 (Consequential Modifications No.1) Order 2001 (SI 2001/1149), art.3 and Sch.1, para.65.

Administration of Drugs in Schedules 2,3,4 and 5

7. —(1) Any person may administer to another any drug specified in Schedule 5.

(2) A doctor or dentist may administer to a patient any drug specified in Schedule 2, 3 or 4.

(3) Any person other than a doctor or dentist may administer to a patient, in accordance with the directions of a doctor or dentist, any drug specified in Schedule 2, 3 or 4.

Production and Supply of Drugs in Schedules 2 and 5

8. —(1) Notwithstanding the provisions of Section 4(1)(a) of the Act—
- (a) a practitioner or pharmacist, acting in his capacity as such, may manufacture or compound any drug specified in Schedule 2 or 5.
- (b) a person lawfully conducting a retail pharmacy business and acting in his capacity as such may, at the registered pharmacy at which he carries on that business, manufacture or compound any drug specified in Schedule 2 or 5.

(2) Notwithstanding the provisions of Section 4(1)(b) of the Act, any of the following persons, that is to say—
- (a) a practitioner;
- (b) a pharmacist;
- (c) a person lawfully conducting a retail pharmacy business;
- (d) the person in charge or acting person in charge of a hospital or nursing home which is wholly or mainly maintained by a public authority out of public funds or by a charity or by voluntary subscriptions;
- (e) in the case of such a drug supplied to her by a person responsible for the dispensing and supply of medicines at the hospital or nursing home, the sister or acting sister for the time being in charge of a ward, theatre or other department in such a hospital or nursing home as aforesaid;
- (f) a person who is in charge of a laboratory the recognised activities of which consist in, or include, the conduct of scientific education or research and which is attached to a university, university college or such a hospital as aforesaid or to any other institution approved for the purpose under this sub-paragraph by the Secretary of State:
- (g) a public analyst appointed under Section 27 of the Food Safety Act, 1990;
- (h) [...]
- (i) a sampling officer within the meaning of Schedule 3 to the Medicines Act, 1968;
- (j) a person employed or engaged in connection with a scheme for testing the quality or amount of the drugs, preparations and appliances supplied under the National Health Service Act 1977 or the National Health Service (Scotland) Act 1978 and the Regulations made thereunder:
- (k) a person authorised by the Pharmaceutical Society of Great Britain for the purposes of Section 108 or 109 of the Medicines Act 1968,

may, when acting in his capacity as such, supply or offer to supply any drug specified in Schedule 2 or 5 to any person who may lawfully have that drug in his possession:

Provided that nothing in this paragraph authorises—
- (i) the person in charge or acting person in charge of a hospital or nursing home, having a pharmacist responsible for the dispensing and supply of medicines, to supply or offer to supply any drug;
- (ii) a sister or acting sister for the time being in charge of a ward,

theatre or other department to supply any drug otherwise than for administration to a patient in that ward, theatre or department in accordance with the directions of a doctor or dentist.

(3) Notwithstanding the provisions of Section 4(1)(b) of the Act, a person who is authorised as a member of a group may, under and in accordance with the terms of his group authority and in compliance with any conditions attached thereto, supply or offer to supply any drug specified in Schedule 2 or 5 to any person who may lawfully have that drug in his possession.

(4) Notwithstanding the provisions of Section 4(1)(b) of the Act, a person who is authorised by a written authority issued by the Secretary of State under and for the purposes of this paragraph and for the time being in force may, at the premises specified in that authority and in compliance with any conditions so specified, supply or offer to supply any drug specified in Schedule 5 to any person who may lawfully have that drug in his possession.

(5) Notwithstanding the provisions of Section 4(1)(b) of the Act—

(a) the owner of a ship, or the master of a ship which does not carry a doctor among the seamen employed in it;

(b) the installation manager of an offshore installation,

may supply or offer to supply any drug specified in Schedule 2 or 5—

(i) for the purpose of compliance with any of the provisions specified in paragraph (6), to any person on that ship or installation;

(ii) to any person who may lawfully supply that drug to him;

(iii) to any constable for the purpose of the destruction of that drug.

(6) The provisions referred to in paragraph (5) are any provision of, or of any instrument which is in force under—

(a) the Merchant Shipping Acts;

(b) the Mineral Workings (Offshore Installations) Act 1971, or

(c) the Health and Safety at Work etc. Act 1974.

AMENDMENT

Subs.(2)(h) repealed by the Food Safety Act 1990 (Consequential Modifications) (No.2) (Great Britain) Order 1990 (SI 1990/2487) reg.5(6).

Production and Supply of Drugs in Schedules 3 and 4

9. —(1) Notwithstanding the provisions of Section 4(1)(a) of the Act—

(a) a practitioner or pharmacist, acting in his capacity as such, may manufacture or compound any drug specified in Schedule 3 or 4;

(b) a person lawfully conducting a retail pharmacy business and acting in his capacity as such may, at the registered pharmacy at which he carries on that business, manufacture or compound any drug specified in Schedule 3 or 4;

(c) a person who is authorised by a written authority issued by the Secretary of State under and for the purposes of this sub-paragraph and for the time being in force may, at the premises specified in that authority and in compliance with any conditions so specified, produce any drug specified in Schedule 3 or 4.

(2) Notwithstanding the provisions of Section 4(1)(b) of the Act, any of the following persons, that is to say—

(a) a practitioner;

(b) a pharmacist;

(c) a person lawfully conducting a retail pharmacy business;

(d) a person in charge of a laboratory the recognised activities of which consist in, or include, the conduct of scientific education or research;

(e) a public analyst appointed under Section 27 of the Food Safety Act, 1990;

(f)   [...]
(g)   a sampling officer within the meaning of Schedule 3 to Medicines Act, 1968;
(h)   a person employed or engaged in connection with a scheme for testing the quality or amount of the drugs, preparations and appliances supplied under the National Health Service Act 1977 or the National Health Service (Scotland) Act 1978 and the Regulations made thereunder;
(i)   a person authorised by the Pharmaceutical Society of Great Britain for the purposes of Section 108 or 109 of the Medicines Act 1968, may, when acting in his capacity as such, supply or offer to supply any drug specified in Schedule 3 or 4 to any person who may lawfully have that drug in his possession.
(3)   Notwithstanding the provisions of Section 4(1)(b) of the Act—
(a)   a person who is authorised as a member of a group, under and in accordance with the terms of his group authority and in compliance with any conditions attached thereto;
(b)   the person in charge or acting person in charge of a hospital or nursing home;
(c)   in the case of such a drug supplied to her by a person responsible for the dispensing and supply of medicines at that hospital or nursing home, the sister or acting sister for the time being in charge of a ward, theatre or other department in a hospital or nursing home,
may, when acting in his capacity as such, supply or offer to supply any drug specified in Schedule 3, or any drug specified in Schedule 4 which is contained in a medicinal product, to any person who may lawfully have that drug in his possession:
Provided that nothing in this paragraph authorises—
(i)   the person in charge or acting person in charge of a hospital or nursing home, having a pharmacist responsible for the dispensing and supply of medicines, to supply or offer to supply any drug;
(ii)   a sister or acting sister for the time being in charge of a ward, theatre or other department to supply any drug otherwise than for administration to a patient in that ward, theatre or department in accordance with the directions of a doctor or dentist.
(4)   Notwithstanding the provisions of Section 4(1)(b) of the Act—
(a)   a person who is authorised by a written authority issued by the Secretary of State under and for the purposes of this sub-paragraph and for the time being in force may, at the premises specified in that authority and in compliance with any conditions so specified, supply or offer to supply any drug specified in Schedule 3 or 4 to any person who may lawfully have that drug in his possession;
(b)   a person who is authorised under paragraph (1)(c) may supply or offer to supply any drug which he may, by virtue of being so authorised, lawfully produce to any person who may lawfully have that drug in his possession.
(5)   Notwithstanding the provisions of Section 4(1)(b) of the Act—
(a)   the owner of a ship, or the master of a ship which does not carry a doctor among the seamen employed in it;
(b)   the installation manager of an offshore installation,
may supply or offer to supply any drug specified in Schedule 3, or any drug specified in Schedule 4 which is contained in a medicinal product—
(i)   for the purpose of compliance with any of the provisions specified in Regulation 8(6), to any person on that ship or installation; or
(ii)   to any person who may lawfully supply that drug to him.
(6)   Notwithstanding the provisions of Section 4(1)(b) of the Act, a person

in charge of a laboratory may, when acting in his capacity as such, supply or offer to supply any drug specified in Schedule 3 which is required for use as a buffering agent in chemical analysis to any person who may lawfully have that drug in his possession.

AMENDMENTS

Subs.(3) substituted by the Misuse of Drugs (Amendment) Regulations 1986 (SI 1986/2330) reg.2(2).

Subs.(2)(e) substituted by the Food Safety Act 1990 (Consequential Modifications) (No.2) (Great Britain) Order 1990 (SI 1990/2487) art.5(c).

Subs.(2)(f) repealed by the Food Safety Act 1990 (Consequential Modifications) (No.2) (Great Britain) Order 1990 (SI 1990/2487) reg.5(6).

Possession of Drugs in Schedules 2, 3 and 4

10. —(1) Notwithstanding the provisions of Section 5(1) of the Act—
(a) a person specified in one of sub-paragraphs (a) to (k) of Regulation 8(2) may have in his possession any drug specified in Schedule 2;
(b) a person specified in one of sub-paragraphs (a) to (i) of Regulation 9(2) may have in his possession any drug specified in Schedule 3 or 4;
(c) a person specified in Regulation 9(3)(b) or (c) or Regulation 9(6) may have in his possession any drug specified in Schedule 3,
for the purpose of acting in his capacity as such a person:
Provided that nothing in this paragraph authorises—
  (i) a person specified in sub-paragraph (e) of Regulation 8(2);
  (ii) a person specified in sub-paragraph (c) of Regulation 9(3); or
  (iii) a person specified in Regulation 9(6),
to have in his possession any drug other than such a drug as is mentioned in the paragraph or sub-paragraph in question specifying him.

(2) Notwithstanding the provisions of Section 5(1) of the Act, a person may have in his possession any drug specified in Schedule 2 or 3 for administration for medical, dental or veterinary purposes in accordance with the directions of a practitioner:
Provided that this paragraph shall not have effect in the case of a person to whom the drug has been supplied by or on the prescription of a doctor if—
(a) that person was then being supplied with any controlled drug by or on the prescription of another doctor and failed to disclose that fact to the first mentioned doctor before the supply by him or on his prescription; or
(b) that or any other person on his behalf made a declaration or statement, which was false in any particular, for the purpose of obtaining the supply or prescription.

(3) Notwithstanding the provisions of Section 5(1) of the Act, a person who is authorised as a member of a group may, under and in accordance with the terms of his group authority and in compliance with any conditions attached thereto, have any drug specified in Schedule 2 or 3 in his possession.

(4) Notwithstanding the provisions of Section 5(1) of the Act—
(a) a person who is authorised by a written authority issued by the Secretary of State under and for the purposes of this sub-paragraph and for the time being in force may, at the premises specified in that authority and in compliance with any conditions so specified, have in his possession any drug specified in Schedule 3 or 4;
(b) a person who is authorised under Regulation 9(1)(c) may have in his possession any drug which he may, by virtue of being so authorised, lawfully produce;
(c) a person who is authorised under Regulation 9(4)(a) may have in his

possession any drug which he may, by virtue of being so authorised, lawfully supply or offer to supply.

(5) Notwithstanding the provisions of Section 5(1) of the Act—

(a) any person may have in his possession any drug specified in Schedule 2 or 3 for the purpose of compliance with any of the provisions specified in Regulation 8(6);

(b) the master of a foreign ship which is in a port in Great Britain may have in his possession any drug specified in Schedule 2 or 3 so far as necessary for the equipment of the ship.

(6) The foregoing provisions of this Regulation are without prejudice to the provisions of Regulation 4(2)(a).

Exemption for Midwives

11. —(1) Notwithstanding the provisions of Sections 4(1)(b) and 5(1) of the Act, a registered midwife who has, in accordance with the provisions of rules made under Section 15(1)(b) of the Act of 1979, notified to the local supervising authority her intention to practise may, subject to the provisions of this Regulation—

(a) so far as necessary to her professional practice, have in her possession;

(b) so far as necessary as aforesaid, administer; and

(c) surrender to the appropriate medical officer such stocks in her possession as are no longer required by her of,

any controlled drug which she may, under and in accordance with the provisions of the Medicines Act, 1968 and of any instrument which is in force thereunder, lawfully administer.

(2) Nothing in paragraph (1) authorises a midwife to have in her possession any drug which has been obtained otherwise than on a midwife's supply order signed by the appropriate medical officer.

(3) In this Regulation, the expression—

"the Act of 1979" means the Nurses, Midwives and Health Visitors Act, 1979;

"appropriate medical officer" means—

(a) a doctor who is for the time being authorised in writing for the purposes of this Regulation by the local supervising authority for the region or area in which the drug was, or is to be, obtained; or

(b) for the purposes of paragraph (2), a person appointed under and in accordance with Section 16 of the Act of 1979 by that authority to exercise supervision over registered midwives within their area, who is for the time being authorised as aforesaid;

"local supervising authority" has the meaning it is given by Section 16(1) of the Act of 1979;

"midwife's supply order" means an order in writing specifying the name and occupation of the midwife obtaining the drug, the purpose for which it is required and the total quantity to be obtained.

Cultivation Under Licence of Cannabis Plant

12. Where any person is authorised by a licence of the Secretary of State issued under this Regulation and for the time being in force to cultivate plants of the genus *Cannabis*, it shall not by virtue of Section 6 of the Act be unlawful for that person to cultivate any such plant in accordance with the terms of the licence and in compliance with any conditions attached to the licence.

Approval of Premises for Cannabis Smoking for Research Purposes

13. Section 8 of the Act (which makes it an offence for the occupier of premises to permit certain activities there) shall not have effect in relation to the smoking of cannabis or cannabis resin for the purposes of research on any premises for the time being approved for the purpose under this Regulation by the Secretary of State.

Documents to be Obtained by Supplier of Controlled Drugs

14. —(1) Where a person (hereafter in this paragraph referred to as "the supplier"), not being a practitioner, supplies a controlled drug otherwise than on a prescription, the supplier shall not deliver the drug to a person who—

(a) purports to be sent by or on behalf of the person to whom it is supplied (hereafter in this paragraph referred to as "the recipient"); and

(b) is not authorised by any provision of these Regulations other than the provisions of Regulations 6(6) and (7)(f) to have that drug in his possession,

unless that person produces to the supplier a statement in writing signed by the recipient to the effect that he is empowered by the recipient to receive that drug on behalf of the recipient, and the supplier is reasonably satisfied that the document is a genuine document.

(2) Where a person (hereafter in this paragraph referred to as "the supplier") supplies a controlled drug, otherwise than on a prescription or by way of administration, to any of the persons specified in paragraph (4), the supplier shall not deliver the drug—

(a) until he has obtained a requisition in writing which—

   (i) is signed by the person to whom the drug is supplied (hereafter in this paragraph referred to as "the recipient");

   (ii) states the name, address and profession or occupation of the recipient;

   (iii) specifies the purpose for which the drug supplied is required and the total quantity to be supplied; and

   (iv) where appropriate, satisfies the requirements of paragraph (5);

(b) unless he is reasonably satisfied that the signature is that of the person purporting to have signed the requisition and that that person is engaged in the profession or occupation specified in the requisition:

Provided that where the recipient is a practitioner and he represents that he urgently requires a controlled drug for the purpose of his profession, the supplier may, if he is reasonably satisfied that the recipient so requires the drug and is, by reason of some emergency, unable before delivery to furnish to the supplier a requisition in writing duly signed, deliver the drug to the recipient on an undertaking by the recipient to furnish such a requisition within the twenty-four hours next following.

(3) A person who has given such an undertaking as aforesaid shall deliver to the person by whom the controlled drug was supplied a signed requisition in accordance with the undertaking.

(4) The persons referred to in paragraph (2) are—

(a) a practitioner;

(b) the person in charge or acting person in charge of a hospital or nursing home;

(c) a person who is in charge of a laboratory;

(d) the owner of a ship, or the master of a ship which does not carry a doctor among the seamen employed on it;

(e) the master of a foreign ship in a port in Great Britain;

(f) the installation manager of an offshore installation.

(5) A requisition furnished for the purposes of paragraph (2) shall—

(a) where furnished by the person in charge or acting person in charge of a hospital or nursing home, be signed by a doctor or dentist employed or engaged in that hospital or nursing home;

(b) where furnished by the master of a foreign ship, contain a statement, signed by the proper officer of the port health authority, or, in Scotland, the medical officer designated under Section 14 of the National Health Service (Scotland) Act 1978 by the Health Board, within whose jurisdiction the ship is, that the quantity of the drug to be supplied is the quantity necessary for the equipment of the ship.

(6) Where the person responsible for the dispensing and supply of medicines at any hospital or nursing home supplies a controlled drug to the sister or acting sister for the time being in charge of any ward, theatre or other department in that hospital or nursing home (hereafter in this paragraph referred to as "the recipient") he shall—

(a) obtain a requisition in writing, signed by the recipient, which specifies the total quantity of the drug to be supplied; and

(b) mark the requisition in such manner as to show that it has been complied with,

and any requisition obtained for the purposes of this paragraph shall be retained in the dispensary at which the drug was supplied and a copy of the requisition or a note of it shall be retained or kept by the recipient.

(7) Nothing in this regulation shall have effect in relation to—

(a) the drugs specified in Schedules 4 and 5 or poppy straw;

(b) any drug specified in Schedule 3 contained in or comprising a preparation which—

(i) is required for use as a buffering agent in chemical analysis,

(ii) has present in it both a substance specified in paragraph 1 or 2 of that Schedule and a salt of that substance, and

(iii) is premixed in a kit.

(c) any exempt product.

AMENDMENTS

Subs.(7) substituted by the Misuse of Drugs (Amendment) Regulations 1988 (SI 1988/916) reg.2(3).

Subs.(7)(c) inserted by the Misuse of Drugs (Amendment) Regulations 1999 (SI 1999/1404) reg.2(4) (effective July 1, 1999).

Form of Prescriptions

15. —(1) Subject to the provisions of this Regulation, a person shall not issue a prescription containing a controlled drug other than a drug specified in Schedule 4 or 5 or temazepam unless the prescription complies with the following requirements, that is to say, it shall—

(a) be in ink or otherwise so as to be indelible and be signed by the person issuing it with his usual signature and dated by him;

(b) insofar as it specifies the information required by sub-paragraphs (e) and (f) below to be specified, be written by the person issuing it in his own handwriting;

(c) except in the case of a health prescription, specify the address of the person issuing it;

(d) have written thereon, if issued by a dentist, the words "for dental treatment only" and, if issued by a veterinary surgeon or a veterinary practitioner, a declaration that the controlled drug is prescribed for an animal or herd under his care;

(e) specify the name and address of the person for whose treatment it is issued or, if it is issued by a veterinary surgeon or veterinary practitioner, of the person to whom the controlled drug prescribed is to be delivered;

(f) specify the dose to be taken and—

    (i) in the case of a prescription containing a controlled drug which is a preparation, the form and, where appropriate, the strength of the preparation, and either the total quantity (in both words and figures) of the preparation or the number (in both words and figures) of dosage units, as appropriate, to be supplied;

    (ii) in any other case, the total quantity (in both words and figures) of the controlled drug to be supplied;

(g) in the case of a prescription for a total quantity intended to be supplied by instalments, contain a direction specifying the amount of the instalments of the total amount which may be supplied and the intervals to be observed when supplying.

(2) Paragraph (1)(b) shall not have effect in relation to—

(a) a prescription issued by a person approved (whether personally or as a member of a class) for the purposes of this paragraph by the Secretary of State; or

(b) a prescription containing no controlled drug other than—

    (i) phenobarbitone;

    (ii) phenobarbitone sodium; or

    (iii) a preparation containing a drug specified in paragraph (i) or (ii) above.

(3) In the case of a prescription issued for the treatment of a patient in a hospital or nursing home, it shall be a sufficient compliance with paragraph (1)(e) if the prescription is written on the patient's bed card or case sheet.

AMENDMENT

Subs.(1) as amended by the Misuse of Drugs (Amendment) (No.2) Regulations 1995 (SI 1995/3244) reg.2(2).

Provisions as to Supply on Prescription

16. —(1) A person shall not supply a controlled drug other than a drug specified in Schedule 4 or 5 on a prescription—

(a) unless the prescription complies with the provisions of Regulation 15;

(b) unless the address specified in the prescription as the address of the person issuing it is an address within the United Kingdom;

(c) unless he either is acquainted with the signature of the person by whom it purports to be issued and has no reason to suppose that it is not genuine, or has taken reasonably sufficient steps to satisfy himself that it is genuine;

(d) before the date specified in the prescription;

(e) subject to paragraph (3), later than thirteen weeks after the date specified in the prescription.

(2) Subject to paragraph (3), a person supplying on prescription a controlled drug other than a drug specified in Schedule 4 or 5 shall, at the time of the supply, mark on the prescription the date on which the drug is supplied and, unless it is a health prescription, shall retain the prescription on the premises from which the drug was supplied.

(3) In the case of a prescription containing a controlled drug other than a drug specified in Schedule 4 or 5, which contains a direction that specified instalments of the total amount may be supplied at stated intervals, the person supplying the drug shall not do so otherwise than in accordance with that direction and—

(a) paragraph (1) shall have effect as if for the requirement contained in subparagraph (e) thereof there were substituted a requirement that the occasion on which the first instalment is supplied shall not be later than thirteen weeks after the date specified in the prescription;

(b) paragraph (2) shall have effect as if for the words "at the time of the supply" there were substituted the words "on each occasion on which an instalment is supplied".

Exemption for Certain Prescriptions

17. Nothing in Regulations 15 and 16 shall have effect in relation to a prescription issued for the purposes of a scheme for testing the quality or amount of the drugs, preparations and appliances supplied under the National Health Service Act, 1977 or the National Health Service (Scotland) Act 1978 and the Regulations made thereunder or to any prescriptions issued for the purposes of the Medicines Act, 1968 to a sampling officer within the meaning of that Act.

AMENDMENT

Section 17 as amended by the Food Safety Act 1990 (Consequential Modifications) (No.2) (Great Britain) Order 1990 (SI 1990/2487) art.5(e).

Marking of Bottles and Other Containers

18. —(1) Subject to paragraph (2), no person shall supply a controlled drug otherwise than in a bottle, package or other container which is plainly marked—

(a) in the case of a controlled drug other than a preparation, with the amount of the drug contained therein;

(b) in the case of a controlled drug which is a preparation—

(i) made up into tablets, capsules or other dosage units, with the amount of each component (being a controlled drug) of the preparation in each dosage unit and the number of dosage units in the bottle, package or other container;

(ii) not made up as aforesaid, with the total amount of the preparation in the bottle, package or other container and the percentage of each of its components which is a controlled drug.

(2) Nothing in this Regulation shall have effect in relation to—

(a) the drugs specified in Schedules 4 and 5 or poppy-straw;

(aa) any drug specified in Schedule 3 contained in or comprising a preparation which—

(i) is required for use as a buffering agent in chemical analysis,

(ii) has present in it both a substance specified in paragraph 1 or 2 of that Schedule and a salt of that substance, and

(iii) is premixed in a kit;

(ab) any exempt product;

(b) the supply of a controlled drug by or on the prescription of a practitioner;

(c) the supply of a controlled drug for administration in a clinical trial or a medicinal test on animals.

(3) In this Regulation, the expressions "clinical trial" and "medicinal test on animals" have the same meanings as in the Medicines Act, 1968.

AMENDMENTS

Subs.(2)(aa) inserted by the Misuse of Drugs (Amendment) Regulations 1988 (SI 1988/916) reg.2(4).

Subs.(2)(ab) inserted by the Misuse of Drugs (Amendment) Regulations 1999 (SI 1999/1404) reg.2(5) (effective July 1, 1999).

Record-keeping Requirements in Respect of Drugs in Schedules 1 and 2

19. —(1) Subject to paragraph (3) and Regulation 21, every person authorised by or under Regulation 5 or 8 to supply any drug specified in Schedule 1 or 2 shall comply with the following requirements, that is to say—

(a) he shall, in accordance with the provisions of this Regulation and of Regulation 20, keep a register and shall enter therein in chronological sequence in the form specified in Part I or Part II of Schedule 6, as the case may require, particulars of every quantity of a drug specified in Schedule 1 or 2 obtained by him and of every quantity of such a drug supplied (whether by way of administration or otherwise) by him whether to persons within or outside Great Britain;

(b) he shall use a separate register or separate part of the register for entries made in respect of each class of drugs, and each of the drugs specified in paragraphs 1 and 3 of Schedule 1 and paragraphs 1, 3 and 6 of Schedule 2 together with its salts and any preparation or other product containing it or any of its salts shall be treated as a separate class, so however that any stereoisomeric form of a drug or its salts shall be classed with that drug.

(2) Nothing in paragraph (1) shall be taken as preventing the use of a separate section within a register or separate part of a register in respect of different drugs of strengths of drugs comprised within the class of drugs to which that register or separate part relates.

(3) The foregoing provisions of this Regulation shall not have effect in relation to—

(a) in the case of a drug supplied to him for the purpose of destruction in pursuance of Regulation 6(2) or (3), a practitioner or pharmacist;

(b) a person licensed under Regulation 5 to supply any drug, where the licence so directs; or

(c) the sister or acting sister for the time being in charge of a ward, theatre or other department in a hospital or nursing home.

Requirements as to Registers

20. Any person required to keep a register under Regulation 19 shall comply with the following requirements, that is to say—

(a) the class of drugs to which the entries on any page of any such register relate shall be specified at the head of that page;

(b) every entry required to be made under Regulation 19 in such a register shall be made on the day on which the drug is obtained or, as the case may be, on which the transaction of the supply of the drug by the person required to make the entry takes place or, if that is not reasonably practicable, on the day next following that day;

(c) no cancellation, obliteration or alteration of any such entry shall be made, and a correction of such an entry shall be made only by way of marginal note or footnote which shall specify the date on which the correction is made;

(d) every such entry and every correction of such an entry shall be made in ink or otherwise so as to be indelible;

(e) such a register shall not be used for any purpose other than the purposes of these Regulations;

(f) a separate register shall be kept in respect of each premises at which the person required to keep the register carries on his business or occupation, but subject to that not more than one register shall be kept at one time in respect of each class of drugs in respect of which he is required to keep a separate register, so, however, that a separate register may, with the approval of the Secretary of State, be kept in respect of each department of the business carried on by him;

(g) every such register in which entries are currently being made shall be kept at the premises to which it relates.

Record-keeping Requirements in Respect of Drugs in Schedule 2 in Particular Cases

21. — (1) Where a drug specified in Schedule 2 is supplied in accordance with Regulation 8(5)(a)(i) to any person on a ship, an entry in the official log book required to be kept under the Merchant Shipping Acts or, in the case of a ship which is not required to carry such an official logbook, a report signed by the master of the ship, shall, notwithstanding anything in these Regulations, be a sufficient record of the supply if the entry or report specifies the drug supplied and, in the case of a report, it is delivered as soon as may be to a superintendent at a Marine Office established and maintained under the Merchant Shipping Acts.

(2) Where a drug specified in Schedule 2 is supplied in accordance with Regulation 8(5)(b)(i) to a person on an offshore installation, an entry in the installation logbook required to be maintained under the Offshore Installations (Logbooks and Registration of Death) Regulations 1972 which specifies the drug supplied shall, notwithstanding anything in these Regulations, be a sufficient record of the supply.

(3) A midwife authorised by Regulation 11(1) to have any drug specified in Schedule 2 in her possession shall—

(a) on each occasion on which she obtains a supply of such a drug, enter in a book kept by her and used solely for the purposes of this paragraph the date, the name and address of the person from whom the drug was obtained, the amount obtained and the form in which it was obtained; and

(b) on administering such a drug to a patient, enter in the said book as soon as practicable the name and address of the patient, the amount administered and the form in which it was administered.

Record-keeping Requirements in Respect of Drugs in Schedules 3 and 4

22. — (1) Every person who is authorised under Regulation 5 or 9(1)(c) to produce any drug specified in Schedule 3 or 4 shall make a record of each quantity of such a drug produced by him.

(2) Every person who is authorised by or under any provision of the Act to import or export any drug specified in Schedule 3 shall make a record of each quantity of such a drug imported or exported by him.

(3) Every person who is authorised under Regulation 9(4) to supply any drug specified in Schedule 4 shall make a record of each quantity of such a drug imported or exported by him.

(4) Paragraph (2) shall not have effect in relation to a person licensed under the Act to import or export any drug where the licence so directs.

Preservation of Registers, Books and Other Documents

23. — (1) All registers and books kept in pursuance of Regulation 19 or 21(3) shall be preserved for a period of two years from the date on which the last entry therein is made.

(2)   Every record made in pursuance of Regulation 22 shall be preserved for a period of two years from the date on which the record was made.

(3)   Every requisition, order or prescription (other than a health prescription) on which a controlled drug is supplied in pursuance of these Regulations shall be preserved for a period of two years from the date on which the last delivery under it was made.

Preservation of Records Relating to Drugs in Schedules 3 and 5

24. — (1) A producer of any drug specified in Schedule 3 or 5 and a wholesale dealer in any such drug shall keep every invoice or other like record issued in respect of each quantity of such a drug obtained by him and in respect of each quantity of such a drug supplied by him.

(2)   A person who is authorised under Regulation 9(4)(a) to supply any drug specified in Schedule 3 shall keep every invoice or other like record issued in respect of each quantity of such a drug obtained by him and in respect of each quantity of such a drug supplied by him.

(3)   A retail dealer in any drug specified in Schedule 3, a person in charge or acting person in charge of a hospital or nursing home and a person in charge of a laboratory shall keep every invoice or other like record issued in respect of each quantity of such a drug obtained by him and in respect of each quantity of such a drug supplied by him.

(4)   A retail dealer in any drug specified in Schedule 5 shall keep every invoice or other like record issued in respect of each quantity of such a drug obtained by him.

(5)   Every invoice or other record which is required by this Regulation to be kept in respect of a drug specified in Schedule 3 shall contain information sufficient to identify the date of the transaction and the person by whom or to whom the drug was supplied.

(6)   Every document kept in pursuance of this Regulation (other than a health prescription) shall be preserved for a period of two years from the date on which it is issued:

Provided that the keeping of a copy of the document made at any time during the said period of two years shall be treated for the purposes of this paragraph as if it were the keeping of the original document.

Exempt Products

24A. Nothing in regulations 19 to 24 shall have effect in relation to any exempt product.

AMENDMENT

Section 24A inserted by the Misuse of Drugs (Amendment) Regulations 1999 (SI 1999/1404), reg.2(6).

Furnishing of Information with Respect to Controlled Drugs

25. — (1) The persons specified in paragraph (2) shall on demand made by the Secretary of State or by any person authorised in writing by the Secretary of State in that behalf—

(a)   furnish such particulars as may be requested in respect of the producing, obtaining or supplying by him of any controlled drug or in respect of any stock of such drugs in his possession;

(b)   for the purpose of confirming any such particulars, produce any stock of such drugs in his possession;

(c) produce any register, book or document required to be kept under these Regulations relating to any dealings in controlled drugs which is in his possession.

(2) The persons referred to in paragraph (1) are—

(a) any person authorised by or under these Regulations to produce any controlled drug;

(b) any person authorised by or under any provision of the Act to import or export any controlled drug;

(c) a wholesale dealer;

(d) a retail dealer;

(e) a practitioner;

(f) the person in charge or acting person in charge of a hospital or nursing home;

(g) a person who is in charge of a laboratory;

(h) a person who is authorised under Regulation 9(4)(a) to supply any controlled drug.

(3) Nothing in this Regulation shall require the furnishing of personal records which a person has acquired or created in the course of his profession or occupation and which he holds in confidence; and in this paragraph "personal records" means documentary and other records concerning an individual (whether living or dead) who can be identified from them and relating to his physical or mental health.

Destruction of Controlled Drugs

26. —(1) No person who is required by any provision of, or by any term or condition of a licence having effect under, these Regulations to keep records with respect to a drug specified in Schedule 1, 2, 3 or 4 shall destroy such a drug or cause such a drug to be destroyed except in the presence of and in accordance with any directions given by a person authorised (whether personally or as a member of a class) for the purposes of this paragraph by the Secretary of State (hereafter in this Regulation referred to as an "authorised person").

(2) An authorised person may, for the purposes of analysis, take a sample of a drug specified in Schedule 1, 2, 3 or 4 which is to be destroyed.

(3) Where a drug specified in Schedule 1, 2 or 4 is destroyed in pursuance of paragraph (1) by or at the instance of a person who is required by any provision of, or by any term or condition of a licence having effect under, these Regulations to keep a record in respect of the obtaining or supply of that drug, that record shall include particulars of the date of destruction and the quantity destroyed and shall be signed by the authorised person in whose presence the drug is destroyed.

(4) Where the master or owner of a ship or installation manager of an offshore installation has in his possession a drug specified in Schedule 2 which he no longer requires, he shall not destroy the drug or cause it to be destroyed but shall dispose of it to a constable, or to a person who may lawfully supply that drug to him.

(5) Nothing in paragraph (1) or (3) shall apply to any person who is required to keep records only by virtue of Regulation 22(2) or (3) or 24(3).

(6) Nothing in paragraph (1) or (3) shall apply to the destruction of a drug which has been supplied to a practitioner or pharmacist for that purpose in pursuance of Regulation 6(2) or (3).

SCHEDULES

SCHEDULE 1

CONTROLLED DRUGS SUBJECT TO THE REQUIREMENTS OF REGULATIONS 14, 15, 16, 18, 19, 20, 23, 25 AND 26

Regulation 3
(1) The following substances and products, namely:
   (a)

Bufotenine	Methcathinone
Cannabinol	Psilocin
Cannabinol derivatives not being	Raw opium
dronabinol or its stereoisomers	Rolicyclidine
Cannabis and cannabis resin	Tenocyclidine
Cathinone	4-Bromo-2,5-dimethoxy-α
Coca leaf	methylphenethylamine
Concentrate of poppy-straw	N,N-Diethyltryptamine
Eticyclidine	N,N-Dimethyltryptamine
Etryptamine	2,5-Dimethoxy-α, 4-
Lysergamide	dimethylphenethylamine
Lysergide and other N-	N-Hydroxy-
alkyl derivatives of lysergamide	tenamphetamine
Mescaline	4-Methyl-aminorex

(b) any compound (not being a compound for the time being specified in sub-paragraph (a) above) structurally derived from tryptamine or from a ring-hydroxy tryptamine by substitution at the nitrogen atom of the sidechain with one or more alkyl substituents but no other substituent;

(c) any compound (not being methoxyphenamine or a compound for the time being specified in sub-paragraph (a) above) structurally derived from phenethylamine, an N-alkylphenethylamine, α-methylphenethylamine, an N-alkyl-α-methylphenethylamine, α-ethylphenethylamine, or an N-alkyl-α-ehtylphenethylamine by substitution in the ring to any extent with alkyl, alkoxy, alkylenedioxy or halide substituents, whether or not further substituted in the ring by one or more other univalent substituents.

(d) any compound (not being a compound for the time being specified in Schedule 2) structurally derived from fentanyl by modification in any of the following ways, that is to say,—
   (i) by replacement of the phenyl portion of the phenethyl group by any heteromonocycle whether or not further substituted in the heterocycle;
   (ii) by substitution in the phenethyl group with alkyl, alkenyl, alkoxy, hydroxy, halogeno, haloalkyl, amino or nitro groups;
   (iii) by substitution in the piperidine ring with alkyl or alkenyl groups;
   (iv) by substitution in the aniline ring with alkyl, alkoxy, alkylenedioxy, halogeno or haloalkyl groups;
   (v) by substitution at the 4-position of the piperdine ring with any alkoxycarbonyl or alkoxyalkyl or acyloxy group;
   (vi) by replacement of the N-propionyl group by another acyl group;

(e) any compound (not being a compound for the time being specified in Schedule 2) structurally derived from pethidine by modification in any of the following ways, that is to say,—
   (i) by replacement of the 1-methyl group by an acyl, alkyl whether or not unsaturated, benzyl or phenethyl group, whether or not further substituted;
   (ii) by substitution in the piperidine ring with alkyl or alkenyl groups or with a propano bridge, whether or not further substituted;
   (iii) by substitution in the 4-phenyl ring with alkyl, alkoxy, aryloxy, halogeno or haloalkyl groups;
   (iv) by replacement of the 4-ethoxycarbonyl by any other alkoxycarbonyl or any alkoxyalkyl or acyloxy group;

    (v) by formation of an N-oxide or of a quaternary base.

(2) Any stereoisomeric form of a substance specified in paragraph (1).

(3) Any ester or ether of a substance specified in paragraph 1 or 2.

(4) Any salt of a substance specified in any of paragraphs 1 to 3.

(5) Any preparation or other product containing a substance or product specified in any of paragraphs 1 to 4, not being a preparation specified in Schedule 5.

AMENDMENTS

Sch.1 as amended by the Misuse of Drugs (Amendment) Regulations 1986 (SI 1986/2330) reg.2(3), the Misuse of Drugs (Amendment) Regulations 1990 (SI 1990/2630) reg.2(a), the Misuse of Drugs (Amendment) Regulations 1995 (SI 1995/2048) reg.2(a) and the Misuse of Drugs (Amendment) Regulations 1998 (SI 1998/882) reg.2(2) (effective from May 1, 1998).

SCHEDULE 2

Regulation 3

CONTROLLED DRUGS SUBJECT TO THE REQUIREMENTS OF REGULATIONS 14,15,16, 18,19,20,21,23,25 AND 26

(1) The following substances and products, namely—

Acetorphine
Alfentanil
Allylprodine
Alphacetylmethadol
Alphameprodine
Alphamethadol
Alphaprodine
Anileridine
Benzethidine
Benzylmorphine
  (3-benzylmorphine)
Betacetylmethadel
Betameprodine
Betamethadol
Betaprodine
Bezitramide
Carfentanil
Clonitazene
Cocaine
Desomorphine
Dextromoramide
Diamorphine
Diampromide
Diethylthiambutene
Difenoxin
Dihydrocodeinone
  O-carboxymethyloxime
Dihydromorphine
Dimenoxadole
Dimepheptanol
Dimethylthiambutene
Dioxaphetyl butyrate
Diphenoxylate
Dipipanone
Dronabinol

Ecgonine, and any derivative of
  ecgonine which is convertible to
  ecgonine or to cocaine
Ethylmethylthiambutene
Etonitazene
Etorphine
Etoxeridine
Fentanyl
Furethidine
Hydrocodone
Hydromorphinol
Hydromorphone
Hydroxypethidine
Isomethadone
Ketobemidone
Levomethorphan
Levomoramide
Levophenacylmorphan
Levorphanol
Lofentanil
Medicinal opium
Metazocine
Methadone
Methadyl acetate
Methyldesorphine
Methyldihydromorphine
  (6-methyldihydromorphine
Metopon
Morpheridine
Morphine
Morphine methobromide, morphine
N-oxide and other pentavelent
nitrogen morphine derivatives
Myrophine
Nicomorphine

Drotebanol
Norlevorphanol
Normethadone
Normorphine
Norpipanone
Oxycodone
Oxymorphone
Pethidine
Phenadoxone
Phenampromide
Phenazocine
Phencyclidine
Phenomorphan
Phenoperidine
Piminodine
Piritramide
Proheptazine
Properidine
Racemethorphan

Noracymethadol
Racemoramide
Racemorphan
Sufentanil
Thebacon
Thebaine
Tilidate
Trimeperidine Zipeprol
4-Cyano-2-dimethylamino-4,4-
     diphenylbutane
4-Cyano-1-methyl-4-
     phenylpiperidine
1-Methyl-4-phenylpiperidine-4-
     carboxylic acid
2-Methyl-3-morpholino-1,1-
     diphenylpropanecarboxylic acid
4-Phenylpiperidine-4-carboxylic
     acid ethyl ester.

(2)   Any stereoisomeric form of a substance specified in paragraph 1 not being dextromethorphan or dextrorphan.

(3)   Any ester or ether of a substance specified in paragraph 1 or 2, not being a substance specified in paragraph 6.

(4)   Any salt of a substance specified in any of paragraphs 1 to 3.

(5)   Any preparation or other product containing a substance or product specified in any of paragraphs 1 to 4, not being a preparation specified in Schedule 5.

(6)   The following substances and products, namely—

Acetyldihydrocodeine
Amphetamine
Codeine
Dextropropoxyphene
Dihydrocodeine
Ethylmorphine
     (3-ethylmorphine)
Fenethylline
Glutethimide
Lefetamine
Mecloqualone

Methaqualone
Methylamphetamine
Methylphenidate
Nicocodine
Nicodicodine
     (6-nicotinoyl-dihydrocodeine)
Norcodeine
Phenmetrazine
Pholcodine
Propiram
Qinalbarbitone

(7)   Any stereoisomeric form of a substance specified in paragraph 6.

(8)   Any salt of a substance specified in paragraph 6 or 7.

(9)   Any preparation or other product containing a substance or product specified in any of paragraphs 6 to 8, not being a preparation specified in Schedule 5.

AMENDMENTS

Sch.2, para.1 as amended by the Misuse of Drugs (Amendment) Regulations 1986 (SI 1986/2330) reg.2(4)(a)(i) and reg.2(4)(a)(ii), the Misuse of Drugs (Amendment) Regulations 1995 (SI 1995/2048) reg.2(6) and the Misuse of Drugs (Amendment) Regulations 1998 (SI 1998/882) reg.2(3) (effective from May 1, 1998).

Sch.2, para.6 as amended by the Misuse of Drugs (Amendment) Regulations 1986 (SI 1986/2330) reg.2(4)(b) and the Misuse of Drugs (Amendment) Regulations 1988 (SI 1988/916) reg.2(5).

Regulation 3   SCHEDULE 3

CONTROLLED DRUGS SUBJECT TO THE REQUIREMENTS OF REGULATIONS 14,15 (EXCEPT TEMAZE-
PAM), 16,18,22,23,24,25 AND 26

(1) The following substances, namely—
     (a)

Benzphetamine	Mephentermine
Buprenorphine	Meprobamate
Cathine	Methylphenobarbitone
Chlorphentermine	Methyprylone
Diethylpropion	Pentazocine
Ethchlorvynol	Phendimetrazine
Ethinamate	Phentermine
Flunitragzepam	Pipradol
Mazindol	Temazepam

(b) any 5,5 disubstituted barbituric acid, not being quinalbarbitone.

(2) Any stereoisomeric form of a substance specified in paragraph 1 not being phenylpropanolamine.

(3) Any salt of a substance specified in paragraph 1 or 2.

(4) Any preparation or other product containing a substance specified in any of paragraphs 1
to 3, not being a preparation specified in Schedule 5.

AMENDMENTS

Subss.(1)(a) and (2) as amended by the Misuse of Drugs (Amendment) Regulations 1986 (SI
1986/2330) reg.2(5).

Subs.(1)(b) as amended by the Misuse of Drugs (Amendment) Regulations 1988 (SI 1988/916)
reg.2(6).

Subs.(1)(a) as amended by the Misuse of Drugs (Amendment) Regulations 1989 (SI 1989/
1460) reg.2(a).

Sch.3 as amended by the Misuse of Drugs (Amendment) (No.2) Regulations 1995 (SI 1995/
3244) reg.2(3)(a).

Subs.(1)(a) as amended by reg.2(3)(b) of the above Regulations and the Misuse of Drugs
(Amendment) Regulations 1998 (SI 1998/882) reg.2(4) (effective May 1, 1998).

Regulation 3   SCHEDULE 4

PART I

CONTROLLED DRUGS EXCEPTED FROM THE PROHIBITION ON POSSESSION WHEN IN THE FORM OF A
MEDICINAL PRODUCT; EXCLUDED FROM THE APPLICATION OF OFFENCES ARISING FROM THE
PROHIBITION ON IMPORTATION AND EXPORTATION WHEN IMPORTED OR EXPORTED IN THE FORM OF
A MEDICINAL PRODUCT BY ANY PERSON FOR ADMINISTRATION TO HIMSELF; AND SUBJECT TO THE
REQUIREMENTS OF REGULATIONS 22, 23, 25 AND 26.

1. The following substances, namely—

Atamestane	Boldenone
Bolandiol	Bolenol
Bolasterone	Bolmantalate
Bolazine	Calusterone
4-Chloromethandienone	Nandrolene
Clostebol	Norboletone

Drostanolone	Norclostebol
Enestebol	Norethandrolone
Epitiostanol	Ovandrotone
Ethyloestrenol	Oxabolone
Fluoxymesterone	Oxandrolone
Formebolone	Oxymesterone
Furazabol	Oxymetholone
Mebolazine	Prasterone
Mepitiostane	Propetandrol
Mesabolone	Quinbolone
Mestanolone	Roxibolone
Mesterolone	Silandrone
Methandienone	Stanolone
Methandriol	Stanozolol
Methenolone	Stenbolone
Methyltestosterone	Testosterone
Metribolone	Thiomesterone
Mibolerone	Trenbolone

2. Any compound (not being Trilostane or a compound for the time being specified in paragraph 1 of this Part of this Schedule) structurally derived from 17-hydroxyandrostan-3-one or from 17-hydroxyestran-3-one by modification in any of the following ways, that is to say,
   (a) by further substitution at position 17 by a methyl or ethyl group;
   (b) by substitution to any extent at one or more of positions 1, 2, 4, 6, 7, 9, 11 or 16, but at no other position;
   (c) by unsaturation in the carbocyclic ring system to any extent, provided that there are no more than two ethylenic bonds in any one carbocyclic ring;
   (d) by fusion of ring A with a heterocyclic system.

3. Any substance which is an ester or ether (or, where more than one hydroxyl function is available, both an ester and an ether) of a substance specified in paragraph 1 or described in paragraph 2 of this Part of this Schedule.

4. The following substances, namely—
   Chorionic Gonadotrophin (HCG)
   Clenbuterol
   Non-human chorionic gonadotrophin
   Somatotropin
   Somatrem
   Somatropin

5. Any stereoisomeric form of a substance specified or described in any of paragraphs 1 to 4 of this Part of this Schedule.

6. Any salt of a substance specified or described in any of paragraphs 1 to 5 of this Part of this Schedule.

7. Any preparation of other product containing a substance or product specified or described in any of paragraphs 1 to 6 of this Part of this Schedule, not being a preparation specified in Schedule 5.

Regulation 3   PART II

CONTROLLED DRUGS EXCEPTED FROM THE PROHIBITION ON IMPORTATION, EXPORTATION AND, WHEN IN THE FORM OF A MEDICINAL PRODUCT, POSSESSION AND SUBJECT TO THE REQUIREMENTS OF REGULATIONS 22, 23, 25 AND 26

(1)   The following substances and products, namely:

Alprazolam	Camazepam
Aminorex	Chlordiazepoxide
Bromazepam	Clobazam
Brotizolan	Clonazepam
Clorazepic acid	Medazepam
Clotiazepam	Mefenorex
Cloxazolam	Mesocarb
Delorazepam	Midazolam
Diazepam	Nimetazepam
Estazolam	Nitrazepam
Ethyl loflazepate	Nordazepam
Fencamfamin	Oxazepam
Fenproporex	Oxazolam
Fludiazepam	Pemoline
Flurazepam	Pinazepam
Halazepam	Prazepam
Haloxazolam	Pyrovalerone
Ketazolam	Tetrazepam
Loprazolam	Triazolam
Lorazepam	N-Ethylamphetamine
Lormetazepam	

(2)   Any stereoisomeric form of a substance specified in paragraph 1.

(3)   Any salt of a substance specified in paragraph 1 or 2.

(4)   Any preparation or other product containing a substance or product specified in any of paragraphs 1 to 3, not being a preparation specified in Schedule 5.

AMENDMENTS

Sch.4, Part II as amended by the Misuse of Drugs (Amendment) Regulations 1986 (SI 1986/2330) reg.2(6), the Misuse of Drugs (Amendment) Regulations 1989 (SI 1989/1460) reg.2(b), the Misuse of Drugs (Amendment) Regulations 1990 (SI 1990/2630) reg.2(b), the Misuse of Drugs (Amendment) Regulations 1995 (SI 1995/2048) reg.2(c), the Misuse of Drugs (Amendment) (No.2) Regulations 1995 (SI 1995/3244) reg.2(4), the Misuse of Drugs (Amendment) Regulations 1998 (SI 1998/882) reg.2(5) (effective from May, 1998).

Sch.4 as amended by the Misuse of Drugs (Amendment) Regulations 1996 (SI 1996/1597) reg.2(5) and reg.2(6).

Regulation 3   SCHEDULE 5

CONTROLLED DRUGS EXCEPTED FROM THE PROHIBITION ON IMPORTATION, EXPORTATION AND POSSESSION AND SUBJECT TO THE REQUIREMENTS OF REGULATIONS 24 AND 25

(1)—[1] Any preparation of one or more of the substances to which this paragraph applies, not being a preparation designed for administration by injection, when compounded with one or more other active or inert ingredients and containing a total of not more than 100 milligrammes of the substance or substances (calculated as base) per dosage unit or with a total concentration of not more than 2.5 per cent. (calculated as base) in undivided preparations.

[2] The substances to which this paragraph applies are acetyldihydrocodeine, codeine, dihydrocodeine, ethylmorphine, nicocodine, nicodicodine (6-nicotinoyldihydrocodeine), norcodeine, pholcodine and their respective salts.

(2)   Any preparation of cocaine containing not more than 0.1 per cent. of cocaine calculated as cocaine base, being a preparation compounded with one or more other active or inert ingredients in such a way that the cocaine cannot be recovered by readily applicable means or in a yield which would constitute a risk to health.

(3)   Any preparation of medicinal opium or of morphine containing (in either case) not more than 0.2 per cent. of morphine calculated as anhydrous morphine base, being a preparation compounded with one or more other active or inert ingredients in such a way that the opium or, as the case may be, the morphine, cannot be recovered by readily applicable means or in a yield which would constitute a risk to health.

(4)   Any preparation of dextropropoxyphene, being a preparation designed for oral administration, containing not more than 135 milligrammes of dextropropoxyphene (calculated as base) per dosage unit or with a total concentration of not more than 2.5 per cent. (calculated as base) in undivided preparations.

(5)   Any preparation of difenoxin containing, per dosage unit, not more than 0.5 milligrammes of difenoxin and a quantity of atropine sulphate equivalent to at least 5 per cent. of the dose of difenoxin.

(6)   Any preparation of diphenoxylate containing, per dosage unit, not more than 2.5 milligrammes of diphenoxylate calculated as base, and a quantity of atropine sulphate equivalent to at least 1 per cent. of the dose of diphenoxylate.

(7)   Any preparation of propiram containing, per dosage unit, not more than 100 milligrammes of propiram calculated as base and compounded with at least the same amount (by weight) of methylcellulose.

(8)   Any powder of ipecacuanha and opium comprising—
     10 per cent. opium, in powder,

MISUSE OF DRUGS (DESIGNATION) ORDER 1986

(SI 1986 No. 2331)

(December 22, 1986)

In pursuance of section 7(4) and (5) of the Misuse of Drugs Act 1971, on the recommendation of the Advisory Council on the Misuse of Drugs, I hereby make the following Order:—

1.— This Order may be cited as the Misuse of Drugs (Designation) Order 1986 and shall come into operation on 1st April 1987.

2.— (1) The controlled drugs specified in Part I of the Schedule hereto are hereby designated as drugs to which Section 7(4), Misuse of Drugs Act 1971, applies.
(2)   Part II of the Schedule hereto shall have effect for the purpose of specifying those controlled drugs which are excepted from Part I thereof.

Article 2   SCHEDULE

PART I

CONTROLLED DRUGS TO WHICH SECTION 7(4) OF THE MISUSE OF DRUGS ACT 1971 APPLIES

(1)   The following substances and products, namely—
    (a)

Bufotenine	Eticyclidine
Cannabinol not being	Etryptamine
dronabinol or its	Lysergamide
stereoisomers	Lysergide and other *N*-alkyl
Cannabinol derivatives	derivatives of lysergamide
Cannabis	Mescaline
Cannabis resin	Methcathinone
Cathinone	Psilocin
Coca leaf	Raw opium
Concentrate of poppy-straw	Rolicyclidine
Tenocyclidine	2,5-Dimethoxy-α,4-
4-Bromo-2,5-dimethoxy-α-	dimethylphenethylamine
methylphenethylamine	*N*-Hydroxy-tenamphetamine
N, N-Diethyltryptamine	4-Methyl-aminorex
N, N-Dimethyltryptamine	

    (b)   any compound (not being a compound for the time being specified in sub-paragraph (a) above) structurally derived from tryptamine or from a ring-hydroxy tryptamine by substitution at the nitrogen atom of the sidechain with one or more alkyl substituents but no other substituent;
    (c)   any compound (not being methoxyphenamine or a compound for the time being specified in sub-paragraph (a) above) structurally derived from phenethylamine, an N-alkylphenethylamine, α-methylphenethylamine, an N-alkyl-α-methylphenethylamine, α-ethylphenethylamine, or an N-alkyl-α-ethylphenethylamine by substitution in the ring to any extent with alkyl, alkoxy, alkylenedioxy or halide substituents,

whether or not further substituted in the ring by one or more other univalent substituents;

(d) any compound (not being a compound for the time being specified in Part II of this Schedule) structurally derived from fentanyl by modification in any of the following ways, that is to say,

(i) by replacement of the phenyl portion of the phenethyl group by any heteromonocycle whether or not further substituted in the heterocycle;

(ii) by substitution in the phenethyl group with alkyl, alkenyl, alkoxy, hydroxy, halogeno, haloalkyl, amino or nitro groups;

(iii) by substitution in the piperidine ring with alkyl or alkenyl groups;

(iv) by substitution in the aniline ring with alkyl, alkoxy, alkylene dioxy, halogeno or haloalkyl groups;

(v) by substitution at the 4-position of the piperidine ring with any alkoxycarbonyl or alkoxyalkyl or acyloxy group;

(vi) by replacement of the N-propionyl group by another acyl group;

(e) any compound (not being a compound for the time being specified in Part II of this Schedule) that is structurally derived from pethidine by modification in any of the following ways, that is to say,—

(i) by replacement of the 1-methyl group by an acyl, alkyl whether or not unsaturated, benzyl or phenethyl group, whether or not further substituted;

(ii) by substitution in the piperidine ring with alkyl or alkenyl groups or with a propano bridge, whether or not further substituted;

(iii) by substitution in the 4-phenyl ring with alkyl, alkoxy, aryloxy, halogeno or haloalkyl groups;

(iv) by replacement of the 4-ethoxycarbonyl by any other alkoxycarbonyl or any alkoxyalkyl or acyloxy group;

(v) by formation of an N-oxide or of a quaternary base.

(2) Any stereoisomeric form of a substance specified in paragraph (1) above.

(3) Any ester or ether of a substance specified in paragraph (1) or (2) above.

(4) Any salt of a substance specified in any of paragraphs (1) to (3) above.

(5) Any preparation or other product containing a substance or product specified in any of paragraphs 1 to 4 above.

PART II

CONTROLLED DRUGS EXCEPTED FROM PART I

(1) The compounds referred to in paragraph 1(d) of Part I of this Schedule are—

Alfentanil	Lofentanil
Carfentanil	Sufentanil

(2) The compounds referred to in paragraph 1(e) of Part I of this Schedule are—

Allylprodine	Betaprodine
Alphameprodine	Hydroxypethidine
Alphaprodine	Properidine
Anileridine	Trimeperidine.
Betameprodine	

AMENDMENTS

Schedule, para.1(a) as amended by the Misuse of Drugs (Designation) (Variation) Order 1990 (SI 1990/2631), the Misuse of Drugs (Designation) (Variation) Order 1995 (SI 1995/2047) art.2 and the Misuse of Drugs (Designation) (Variation) Order 1998 (SI 1998/881) art.2(2) (effective from May 1, 1998).

THE CONTROLLED DRUGS (SUBSTANCES USEFUL FOR MANUFACTURE) (INTRA-COMMUNITY TRADE) REGULATIONS 1993

(SI 1993 No. 2166)

(October 6, 1993)

. . .

In exercise of the powers conferred upon me by section 2(2) of the European Communities Act 1972, I hereby make the following Regulations:

1. These Regulations may be cited as the Controlled Drugs (Substances Useful for Manufacture) (Intra-Community Trade) Regulations 1993 and shall come into force on 6th October 1993.

2. In these Regulations—
"the 1990 Act" means the Criminal Justice (International Co-operation) Act 1990;
"operator" means any person engaged in the manufacture, processing, trade or distribution of scheduled substances in any member State or involved in other related activities such as the brokering and storage of scheduled substances;
"placing on the market" means any supply to a person in any member State, whether against payment or free of charge, of scheduled substances manufactured in a member State or put into free circulation in any member State; and
"scheduled substance", except in so far as the context otherwise requires, means any substance specified in Schedule 1 below, including mixtures containing such substances, but excluding medicinal products or other preparations containing scheduled substances in such a way that such substances cannot be easily used or recovered by readily applicable means.

3. Subject to Regulation 7 below, the obligations imposed on operators by Regulation 4 below shall be treated as if they were requirements imposed on them by regulations made under Section 13(1) of the 1990 Act, and as if the references in Regulation 4 to scheduled substances were references to scheduled substances within the meaning of Part II of that Act.

. . .

5. —(1) No operator shall manufacture or place on the market any of the scheduled substances specified in Category 1 of Schedule 1 below without a licence to do so granted by the Secretary of State in accordance with Regulation 6(1) below.
(2) An operator who holds a licence granted under paragraph (1) above shall not supply any of the substances there referred to, except to any of the following persons—
(a) another operator holding such a licence;
(b) an operator who requires any such substance for the manufacture of a medicinal product and in respect of whom a licence is in force to manufacture that product under Section 8(2) of the Medicines Act 1968;
(c) a pharmacist or a person lawfully conducting a retail pharmacy business in accordance with Section 69 of the Medicines Act 1968;
(d) a person who is in charge of a laboratory, the recognised activities of which consist in, or include, the conduct of scientific education or re-

search, and which is attached to a university or a hospital in the United Kingdom or to any other institution approved for the purpose by the Secretary of State;

(e) any other person who has been authorised by the Secretary of State to be supplied with such a substance for the purposes of the manufacture of non-medicinal products or other special purposes; or

(f) any other person permitted by a member State other than the United Kingdom to be supplied with, possess or handle such substances in accordance with Article 4(3) of Council Directive 92/109/EEC.

(3) An operator involved in the manufacture or placing on the market of scheduled substances listed in Category 2 of Schedule 1 below shall register with the Secretary of State the addresses of the premises from which he manufactures or trades in such substances and shall notify him in writing of any change of address.

(4) In this regulation—

"medicinal product" has the meaning assigned to it by Section 130 of the Medicines Act 1968, and "non-medicinal products" shall be construed accordingly; and

"pharmacist" has the meaning assigned to it by Section 132(1) of that Act.

6. — (1) In considering whether to grant a licence under Regulation 5(1) above, the Secretary of State shall take into account in particular the competence and integrity of the applicant for that licence.

(2) A licence granted under Regulation 5(1) above may be revoked or suspended by the Secretary of State where there are reasonable grounds for belief that the holder of that licence is no longer a fit and proper person to hold it, or that the conditions under which it was granted are no longer fulfilled.

7. Where a person is convicted of an offence contrary to Section 13(5) of the 1990 Act as a result of the application of Regulation 3 above, Section 13(5)(a) of the Act shall have effect as if for the words "6 months" there were substituted the words "3 months".

8. — (1) A person who fails to comply with any provision of Regulation 5 above is guilty of an offence and liable—

(a) on summary conviction, to imprisonment for a term not exceeding 3 months or a fine not exceeding the statutory maximum or both;

(b) on conviction on indictment, to imprisonment for a term not exceeding two years or a fine or both.

(2) The powers conferred by subsection (1) of Section 23 of the Misuse of Drugs Act 1971 shall be exercisable also for the purposes of the execution of Regulation 5 above and subsection (3) of that section (excluding paragraph (a)) shall apply also to the offence under paragraph (1) above, taking references in those subsections to controlled drugs as references to scheduled substances.

(3) The reference in paragraph (1) above to a person who fails to comply with any provision in Regulation 5 above includes a person, who in purported compliance with any such provision—

(a) furnishes information which he knows to be false in a material particular; or

(b) recklessly furnishes information which is false in a material particular.

Regulation 2   SCHEDULE

SCHEDULED SUBSTANCES

CATEGORY I

Ephedrine	Lysergic acid
Ergometrine	3, 4 methylenedioxyphenyl
Ergotamine	propan-2-one
Isosafrole	N-acetylanthranilic acid
I-phenyl-2-propanone	Psedoephedrine
Piperonal	Safrole

The salts of the substances listed in this Category whenever the existence of such salts is possible.

CATEGORY 2

Acetic anhydride	Phenylacetic acid
Anthranilic acid	Piperidine

The salts of the substances listed in this Category whenever the existence of such salts is possible.

CRIMINAL JUSTICE (SCOTLAND) ACT 1987 (CROWN SERVANTS AND REGULATORS ETC.) REGULATIONS 1994

(SI 1994 No. 1808)

(July 6, 1994)

The Secretary of State, in exercise of the powers conferred on him by section 46A(1) to (5) of the Criminal Justice (Scotland) Act 1987 and of all other powers enabling him in that behalf, hereby makes the following Regulations:

Citation and commencement

1. These Regulations may be cited as the Criminal Justice (Scotland) Act 1987 (Crown Servants and Regulators Etc.) Regulations 1994 and shall come into force on 1st August 1994.

Interpretation

2. In these Regulations—
"the Act" means the Criminal Law (Consolidation) (Scotland) Act 1995;
"relevant financial business" has the meaning given by Regulation 4 of the Money Laundering Regulations 1993.

Application of the Act to Director of Savings and staff

3. Sections 36, 37, 38, 39 and 40 of the Act (offences in connection with proceeds of drug trafficking) shall apply to the following persons, namely—
(a) the Director of Savings; and
(b) any person employed by or otherwise engaged in the service of the Director of Savings;
in circumstances where the said Director or any such person is carrying on relevant financial business.

Designation of persons appearing to the Secretary of State to be performing regulatory etc. functions

4. — (1) Section 39 of the Act (failure to disclose knowledge or suspicion of money laundering) shall not apply to the following persons, being hereby designated for the purposes of paragraph (a) of Section 42(2) of the Act—
(a) the Bank of England;
(b) the Building Societies Commission;
(c) a designated agency within the meaning of the Financial Services Act 1986;
(d) a recognised self-regulating organisation within the meaning of the Financial Services Act 1986;
(e) a recognised self-regulating organisation within the meaning of the Financial Services Act 1986;
(f) a transferee body within the meaning of the Financial Services Act 1986;
(g) a recognised self-regulating organisation for friendly societies within the meaning of the Financial Services Act 1986;
(h) the Council of Lloyds;
(i) the Friendly Societies Commission;
(j) the Chief Registrar of Friendly Societies;
(k) the Assistant Registrar of Friendly Societies for Scotland;

(l)   the Central Office of the Registry of Friendly Societies;
(m) the Register of Friendly Societies for Northern Ireland;
(n)   the Assistant Registrar of Credit Unions for Northern Ireland.

(2)   The following category of persons is hereby prescribed for the purposes of paragraph (b) of Section 42(2) of the Act, namely, persons who are (for the purpose of performing regulatory, supervisory, investigative or registration functions) employed by or otherwise engaged in the service of any person designated under paragraph (1) of this Regulation.

(3)   Section 39 of the Act shall not apply in any circumstances to any person who falls within a category of persons prescribed for the purposes of paragraph (b) of Section 42(2) of the Act.

INDEX

References are to page number